POCATELLO
THE STARTING PLACE
OF GRACE

Pocatello: The Starting Place of Grace is a work of nonfiction. Some names of living and deceased characters have been changed.

Bible quotations are taken from the *Life Application Study Bible*, which is the New King James Version of the Bible, ©1993 by Tyndale House Publishers, INC.

Alcoholics Anonymous (AA) references are taken from the (https://www.aa.org/) online versions of *The Big Book (Alcoholics Anonymous)*, and *The Twelve Steps and Twelve Traditions*.

Personal Photos Supplied by Presley Louis Vann Sr.

ISBN: 978-1-998315-22-2
        978-1-998315-27-7

Published by Inicio Press
iniciopress.com

Pocatello

POCATELLO

THE STARTING PLACE OF GRACE

PRESLEY VANN

Presley Louis Vann Sr.

CONTENTS

DEDICATION

This memoir is dedicated to my loving mother, Lillie "Sister" Vann, for keeping her spirit-filled, redeeming light shining upon me. To my lovely wife, Deborah Vann, who, by God's grace, has embraced our matrimonial vows within her heart for fifty-plus years. To my biblically grounded sister, Mildred Wash, who maintained long-distance vigilant prayer over me with our prayerful mother throughout the decades. To my kind-hearted sister, Vivian Cody, who always exhibited a genuine, compassionate concern for me. To Mrs. Idaho Purce, a consistently honorable example of how to keep forging forward despite the obstacles and hurdles of racial discrimination and segregation. And to *Mi Señor Jesucristo, Wǒ de zhǔ yēsū jīdū, Мой Господь Иисус Христос, Мій Господь Ісус Христос, Naui Ju Yesu Geuliseudo, Rabiy Yasue Almasih, my Lord Jesus Christ.*

Alfred and Lillie Vann

1

FROM BASEMENT TO PROJECTS

Life Started in a Dungeon

My name is Presley L. Vann. I was born May 2, 1950, in Pocatello, Idaho, to Alfred James Vann Senior., a half-Black, half-Cherokee Indian father from Chelsea, Oklahoma. My father spent his early life growing up on a segregated Cherokee Indian reservation in Oklahoma. My Mother, Lillie Ziola Vann, of Little Rock, Arkansas, grew up with the lingering history of slave plantation life in Arkansas. So, did my parents retain any unfavorable biases that affected how they raised their baby son because of the vividly contrasting ethnic environments they'd been exposed to?

I recall a joyful childhood listening to songs on the radio like "How Much Is That Doggie in the Window?" by Patti Page, "Pretend" by Nat King Cole, and "You, You, You" by the Ames Brothers, as well as country and western songs like "Your Cheatin' Heart" by Hank Williams, "It's Been So Long" by Webb Pierce, and R & B hits like "Shake a Hand" by Faye Adams and "Money Honey" by Clyde McPhatter. These began a long soundtrack that ran throughout my life.

I can still see my mom's shadow moving about from the light leaking through the basement windows fixed at the top of the wall of our subterranean dwelling. Her shadow would disappear as it crossed the doorway to the crumbling concrete stairs leading out of what could best be described as a dungeon, where the main area consisted of a cold concrete floor surrounded by four cold concrete walls, with two walls containing unframed doorways that led to a bedroom and bathroom. A farmhouse sink was attached to a corner wall, and on the opposite wall were a coal-wood burning stove and an original ice box for refrigeration.

From the Basement to the Projects

We eventually moved out of the dungeon and into the projects when I was between four and five years old. The projects were buildings constructed for military government housing, but they were put up for sale after the war. The part of the projects we lived in comprised three buildings that formed a "U" shape, with the open-end facing 4th Street. Each building contained four apartments.

Moving from that dim, dingy basement was a literal change from darkness to light. Still, my mom and sister had to share one bedroom, and my father, brother, and I shared the other. The kitchen had a large sink with storage cabinets on both sides, top and bottom. There was an electric refrigerator with a top freezer and a stove with a real oven, all situated in a kitchenette-dining area. The living room had a large oil heater, and a light centered in the middle of the ceiling. Natural light beamed through the windows spaced about the kitchenette-dining and living room areas. This place seemed like heaven compared to the damp basement crypt.

On Sunday mornings, we attended Bethel Baptist Church on the corner of 5th and Fremont. I do not remember my dad attending church with us. It is difficult to describe my dad. Looking back, he was a maze of contradictions. For instance, he stressed working hard and progressing but balked about buying a house. I sensed that my dad constantly frustrated our mother, but I found him exciting, and I simply loved him. I also recall attending bible studies and special church events with my mother and siblings throughout the week. I especially loved attending church during the holidays when we performed in holiday programs and ate lots of tasty holiday food.

Growing up, my mother read the bible to us children. I distinctly remember her reading the Proverbs and the Psalms. She impressed upon us to remember the Lord's Prayer, Matthew 6:9–11, and especially Psalm 23. Mom understood the supernatural power that exists in the Word of God. Later, the 23rd Psalm brought me great comfort and peace in times of trouble and despair, especially verse 4: "Yea, though I walk through the valley of the shadow of death, I will fear no evil; For You are with me; Your rod and Your staff, they comfort me...."

In the dungeon, we had a radio and a small suitcase-shaped record player. But in the projects, our mother got a modern console radio/record player. The console had great sound quality, and my mother could stack multiple records on the record player's spindle. On the record player, we listened to great gospel albums like "Touch Me Lord Jesus" by The Angelic Gospel Singers, "Lead Me, Guide Me," and "Precious Lord" by Brother Joe May. On the console radio, we listened to popular songs at the time, like "Rock Around the Clock" by Bill Haley & His Comets, "The Great Pretender" by The Platters, and "Love Is a Many-Splendored Thing" by The Four Aces.

Despite our family's upgraded lifestyle, we faced segregation in Pocatello. Minorities were restricted to living in an area known as "The Triangle." The Triangle's street borders ran from Center Street to the south and Pocatello Avenue to the west, merging into 1st Street at the southwest corner. Eighth Street ran east, merging with Pocatello Avenue into Oak Street at the northwest corner. We lived on the block of 4th and Lander in the "Hot Zone" of The Triangle.

Some Black families lived in nice houses in the northwestern section of The Triangle financed through the VA. Accompanying segregated housing was unfair employment. Both directly affected my mom and dad. My parents had moved from the Kansas-Missouri area to Denver, Colorado, and eventually settled in Pocatello, Idaho, in December of 1942. My father worked for the Civil Service. Since he was not a member of the armed forces, he didn't qualify for VA benefits.

Dad was a handsome, black-haired man with dark brown skin. Although he was a formally trained machinist, he worked as a welder at the Army airfield on the outskirts of Pocatello. After the Korean War and the Civil Service dissolved, my father became a laborer for the Union Pacific Railroad. In time, he was upgraded to a fuel oil pumper, but he never secured a job as a machinist.

My mother was a lovely Southern woman with light-brown skin. She was a hairdresser who pressed and curled Black women's hair in Pocatello. She also cooked, ironed clothes, and cleaned house for the Markhams, who were a prominent yet genuinely nice White family in Pocatello.

My pre-school days were fun filled since several Black kids my age lived in the neighborhood. In the morning, as soon as I was up and dressed, I went outside to play with whomever, doing whatever. When outside, I was restricted to staying within calling distance of our apartment. Mom said, "Boy, if I call and you don't show up, then while you are out there, doing whatever you're doing, you better give your heart to God because your butt belongs to me when you get home!"

On occasions when I was allowed to leave our project area, I could only go to my older sister Vivian's house or one of my friend's houses. When I arrived at my destination, my sister or my friend's mother would call my mom to let her know that I had arrived. When I left, my friend's mother or my sister would call my mom, so she knew to expect me home shortly after that.

Mom implemented this protocol because she had trust issues. There were times I'd sneaked off or didn't go home when I was supposed to. When plotting what I viewed as a great escape, it was to get out from under my mother's watchful eye and venture into restricted places. My timing had to be perfect when I did this. I set my internal alarm, so I'd know when to hightail it back to the projects before my mother started calling me. I took such a big risk to make my way down to the Jim Dandy Club, located on the corner of 3rd and Lander in the heart of The Triangle "Hot Zone." From the time I was five, the Jim Dandy Club was my favorite escape destination.

I would rush across Lander Street, then across 3rd Street, to arrive at the corner of the Jim Dandy Club. There, I'd wait anxiously, hoping to see one or two of the voluptuous Black working girls leaning against the wall smoking cigarettes. When I walked down the sidewalk in front of them, they would say things like, "Hey, sugar boy, whatcha up to?" Their sultry words set my soul on fire.

CHAPTER

2

THE JIM DANDY CLUB

When I sneaked down to the Club, I had to be extra careful not to be seen by any of my mom's friends. All the "straight arrow" Black folks in Pocatello hated the Jim Dandy Club with a passion because it was the center of crime and corruption. Mom used to threaten me in her uniquely Southern way, saying, "Boy, if I catch you down at that place, I'm going to beat you like a runaway slave that stole a government mule, and ya rode it hard and put it up wet!"

I must make something clear. Although Mom was a great, loving, and caring mother, from time to time, she talked more harshly to me compared to how she spoke to my siblings, probably because I was flat-out hard-headed. She was deeply concerned about me staying away from the Club because a lot of illegal activities occurred there while the police looked the other way.

The Club owner, Clide, had a brother who lived in Seattle, Washington. Clide also had a nephew, Harrison, who lived in Pocatello. Harrison and I frequently hung out together, and as I grew older and my presence at the Club became more regular, I began to learn the truth about the place. In the late sixties, after my father died, Harrison and I traveled a couple of times to Seattle on the Union Pacific Railroad passenger train. On those trips, I discovered that prostitutes and contraband were traveling between Seattle and Pocatello; the trips were well-planned and kept under the radar of the authorities. The prostitutes arrived in Pocatello with lots of luggage, some containing drugs and weapons.

In my pre-high school years, I had to be extremely careful when I ventured down to the Club because I was the only neighborhood kid my age sneaking around. I would also see some White guys at the Club, and occasionally, I saw the father of one of my schoolmates. The Club was a busy place, and it was easy to sneak down the hallway to peek into the bar or go up and down the stairs to the rooms to see what I could see.

By high school, I became a regular at the Jim Dandy Club and no longer had to sneak around. I would spend more time at the Jim Dandy Club despite the abrasive way Clide treated me. I think he was so harsh to me because of the disdain my mother and many other Black folks in town felt toward the Club. He tolerated me because of the older Black guys I hung out with who made money for him. Although I despised him, the guy had a beautiful family. His wife was a lovely, light-skinned lady with two nice-looking sons and three lovely daughters. The oldest son was my brother's age and was a city and state-awarded athlete. I attended school with the oldest daughter, and I was crazy about her.

The Blacksmith's Barn

Another off-limit hangout was the fascinating yet extremely dangerous Blacksmith's Barn. It was a grand old barn with two massive sliding doors. It was a terribly busy and dangerous place with all the wagons, horses, and vehicles. I would sneak down and look inside in amazement. I was fascinated by the roar of the huge blast furnace, the loud clanging of the blacksmith's hammer, and the clamor of the overhead rotating chain system.

It was especially exciting to be close to the horses. I particularly loved the Clydesdale teams. Being a little guy at the time, I was amazed by how massive and magnificent the animals were. Once, the handlers asked if I wanted to pet one of the gigantic horses. When I eagerly nodded, he pulled down on the reins, bringing the horse's huge head down to my level. My heart felt like it was ready to explode out of my chest as I stroked the side of its face.

I loved going to that old barn when the horses were being trimmed and shod, and especially when the cowboys rode their horses into town. They wore chaps and spurs and carried six-shooters, and sometimes, they showed off their quick draw and finger-twirling techniques with their guns.

The Shag Nasties

Another out-of-bounds destination was a house behind the Jim Dandy Club, where a strange gypsy-type family lived that everybody called the "Shag Nasties." They were a weird group of five to six men and women who drove around town in an old beat-up truck they used for collecting scrap and junk. I would sneak over to the house to window-peek. These folks were strange. Winter or summer, they left their windows open, and you could hear them talking and yelling in their foreign language. Sometimes, I would see one of the men walking around naked, yelling, and throwing things around. Once, I saw the big guy walking around naked, and he grabbed one of the women, laid her over a table, and did his business with her. Still wearing no underwear or socks, he put on his overalls and shoes and met the others at the front door to leave. When they headed out the front door, I took off before they saw me.

Life in the Projects

The projects could be a fairly rough place. There was a large family of sixteen—a dad and mom, eight girls and six boys—and they occupied an entire project building along the alley. The kids covered a wide range of ages, and there was a constant battle for territorial supremacy. I pretty much got along with the whole family, but occasionally, one of the younger boys would stir up some trouble. Then, the boneheaded boy would run home, and shortly after, the entire family would pour out of both ends of the building, scattering like roaches.

A new family moved in across from us. There was a dad, a mom, two boys, and a girl. One day, I saw the older son in the middle of the project's courtyard. I slowly walked up to him, and before I could say a word, he punched me in the gut and took off running as I doubled over and hit the ground. After I recovered, I got up and staggered back to my apartment. My mom and dad were home, but I avoided them. I found my brother and told him what happened. I had the world's best big brother. He was two years older than me, and we called him Junior because he was named after our father, Alfred James Vann, Senior.

I wanted to rush out, look for the kid, and beat the stuffing out of him, but Junior had a better idea. He said the kid would see us if we rushed him, and then he'd probably run back into his apartment. He decided we'd go out our back door, hide at the corner of the kid's building, and wait for him. Junior's plan worked perfectly. The kid soon came out of the apartment's front door with his younger brother and looked around. We let them walk to the middle of the courtyard, and then we rushed them. We positioned ourselves between them and the front door of their apartment, so they had no path for retreat.

Junior walked up to the older brother and asked him. "Why did you hit my brother?"

The kid took a swing at Junior, but Junior dodged the punch and tagged the kid on the side of his face. The fight was on. Pretty soon, I saw our father and the father of the two boys come out of the apartments. Then I saw one of the most amazing things I had ever seen. I thought the dads would start quarreling and come to blows themselves. Instead, they walked up to each other, shook hands, introduced themselves, and started talking while their sons were duking it out and rolling around on the ground. The dads continued talking to each other, glancing now and then at the boys rolling around on the ground, trading punches. After what seemed like an eternity, the two dads finished their conversation and stopped the fight. They made the four of us introduce ourselves and shake hands, which is how we officially met the boys. We went on to become close friends.

My brother, Alfred, Jr. and me

Over time, I forged a tight relationship with the oldest boy. Although he was the same age as my brother, we shared the same devious interests. Their dad was an interesting character. He was a medium height, thickly built man with broad shoulders, muscular arms, and large, thick vice-grip hands. He reminded me of the Marvel rock-skin mutant "Thing." He was a big-rig truck driver for a salvage company on South 2nd Street in Pocatello.

The salvage company would become a familiar place for me down the road. During high school, I worked on several profitable salvage operations for the company. The company's owner was a great, high-spirited guy. He was among the White guys I frequently saw at the Jim Dandy Club, often with a new crew of prostitutes from Seattle, though I never witnessed him hooking up with any of the prostitutes.

My pre-school and elementary school years were wonderful growing up in the projects. The start of elementary school coincided with my introduction to organized recreational sports. I had always loved baseball, but my passion for the sport took off when I started attending Bonneville Elementary School. The recreational sports system in Pocatello was a blessing for all the kids in town, but it was a special blessing for The Triangle kids. Playing recreational sports around town at different parks and fields allowed me to forge close friendships with several White boys, and it was amazing to me when some of them invited me to their homes.

I also invited some of my White friends to come home with me to The Triangle, but none accepted my invitation. I wondered why they would not come with me. Not completely understanding the racial disparity in Pocatello at such early age, I figured they were not allowed to go to The Triangle area by their parents. I did not worry about it and moved on with my new friends. However, as time passed and I matured with my new White friends, I noticed something peculiar about some of their parents.

My White friends' families covered the entire income spectrum. The fathers were straightforward with me whenever I met them. They would greet me, and I felt they treated me fairly, but some mothers treated me differently. It seemed like the mothers at the low end and high end of the income spectrum treated me fairly, but the mothers in the middle of the income spectrum were usually emotionally cold toward me.

It felt like they did not like me, and they did not try to hide it. Many of these mothers were Mormons. They allowed me to enter their houses with their sons, but I never truly felt welcome. I encountered several of these perplexing mothers but returned to their houses anyway. I returned because my mother told me that the bible said that I should display my gentleness whenever I could. I also returned to spite them. I had become a mentally tough little kid from living in The Triangle environment. I was also influenced by hanging out at the lowly speakeasies.

One frigid winter evening during junior high school, I stopped by Clide's house to leave a stuffed animal as a Christmas present for the older daughter. I knocked on the door, and much to my disappointment, Clide answered the door and said, "What the hell do you want?"

I told him I wanted to leave a gift for his oldest daughter. When I tried to hand it to him, he took it from me, tossed it out in the yard, and said, "I ain't giving her nothing from you, and you better get your little Black a** away from here and don't ever come knocking on my door again!"

I turned around and started walking back down the sidewalk toward home. I didn't bother to pick up the stuffed animal; I just walked away feeling broken.

As I walked, I began plotting my revenge against Clide and his 6'3", 265 lbs. of Bluto-from-*Popeye* ugly. Much later, I would exact my revenge against him, but at great personal expense for someone else.

After high school, his oldest daughter worked at the Club. I frequently visited her and spent as much time as possible talking to her. However, because of Clide, I never told her how crazy I was about her.

CHAPTER
3

THE SPEAKEASIES

One day, I went with my dad to a popular speakeasy called Tiny's. After we had been there for a while, the father of our new neighbor showed up. My dad greeted him, and then he introduced him to Tiny and all the Black guys who were there. I was surprised to see the new dad, but I soon discovered that my dad had invited him. His presence made me realize that it was something special to meet at a speakeasy to talk, joke, listen to the blues, and drink. I saw the same camaraderie whenever I was with my dad at any of the speakeasies. When I was at the speakeasies, I usually sat somewhere out of the way and consumed the atmosphere. Over time, a false and twisted sense of admiration affected my thinking and introduced jaded elements to my character.

There were some speakeasies on South 2nd Street in Pocatello, but I mainly went to all the Lander area speakeasies with my father. Sometimes, my dad helped folks with personal or business matters, and this occurred mostly at Tiny's, Pete Morgan's, or May Collins. We never went to the Jim Dandy Club, and I believe it's because the environment at the Club lacked the speakeasy atmosphere, and I don't think my dad wanted to give Clide any of his money.

The speakeasies we frequented were around the Lander Street area between 5th Street and Pocatello Avenue. There were the sisters, Tiny's, and Paralee's. Then there were May Collins, Pete Morgan's, J. D. Harris's, Blare's, and last (but definitely not least) Eddy and Kerry Howell's. The speakeasies' business activities included drinking, drug dealing, poker, shooting craps, bootlegging, and loan sharking. All of them shared prostitutes from the Jim Dandy Club, and periodically, some of them sold some tasty food. Eddy and Kerry Howell's was probably the most stylish speakeasy, serving a variety of folks and big-money players from all over Pocatello and surrounding areas. Unlike the other speakeasies, the Howells had rooms upstairs to accommodate prostitutes.

The next most profitable speakeasy was probably May Collins. She, too, drew folks from all over Pocatello and surrounding areas, but unlike the others, she drew a lot of students and professors from the university.

After May Collins, Blair's would probably come next. Blair had the largest gambling base of high-stakes White men playing in big dollar pots, and you didn't see recreational poker players. He served no food but peddled shots of expensive cognac to his high rollers.

Tiny's and Pete Morgan's had the same type of business setup. They were open every day of the week and were extremely popular and profitable. Each had one main room where everyone sat, drank, smoked, and shot the bull. Their places were not big enough for gambling, but they both had a room the size of a broom closet for an occasional prostitute. They sold a traditional holiday plate with turkey, dressing, and all the trimmings during Thanksgiving and Christmas.

J. D. Harris was a small, hole-in-the-wall dancing and eatery place. You could get a plate with a couple of BBQ ribs or fried chicken, and sometimes a plate of chitlins and collard greens with a couple of pieces of white bread or sometimes a chunk of sweet cornbread. Now and then, he served fried fish, pork chops, or some fairly good meatloaf with brown gravy. J. D. Harris was a great cook. However, he had a dark side as a hypocritical ordained Baptist minister. In the end, he was an old, clever hustler.

Finally, at the end of the line was Paralee's. Paralee was one of Tiny's three sisters in Pocatello. Her business was not a typical speakeasy. She ran a 24/7 knock-on-the-door to buy a bottle of booze, a bottle of wine, or a bag of weed. Since Idaho state liquor stores closed at 8 p.m. on weekdays and Saturdays and closed on Sundays and holidays, Paralee's business thrived outside the other speakeasies, especially when the more regular speakeasies closed in the wee hours. Her clientele included locals, Indians, winos, hippies, college students, and people who normally wouldn't go to the other speakeasies. She made a lot of money, and I often wondered if she ever slept, given her 24/7 operation.

My mom didn't know when we went to the speakeasies, but she heard about our visits from different people. Being a formally trained machinist and welder and a great self-taught mechanic, my father traveled all over Pocatello doing various odd jobs and doing favors for many people, which provided abundant opportunities for us to visit the speakeasies.

My mother called the speakeasies "hell holes of iniquity and ill-repute," and much later in my life, I realized that my mother was dead on. Back then, though, I loved going to the speakeasies with my dad and became totally immersed in what I thought was a great atmosphere. An extremely diverse crowd was drawn to the seedy side of The Triangle by the beckoning sound of the blues, the endless flow of booze, easy access to drugs, the call of shuffling cards and rolling dice, and the lustful beckoning of voluptuous prostitutes.

Pocatello was a remarkably diverse place. First, it was a university town with faculty and students from all over the world. Second, it was a railroad town with a busy passenger line from Omaha, Nebraska, to Seattle, Washington, with passenger trains running morning and afternoon. On the southern end of town was a freight switching yard, and on the opposite end of town was a busy roundhouse that serviced train engines from throughout the western states.

Pocatello also had a sprinkling of industry with the J.R. Simplot fertilizer company, the FMC phosphorus-producing facility, and the Naval Ordnance Plant, where big guns from all the military services were overhauled. Several Pocatello residents worked at the National Reactor Testing Station in the Arco desert, and several worked at the Army Air Force Base, including my father.

I especially enjoyed meeting musicians who came to town to perform, the porters and waiters who served on the Union Pacific passenger line, and the professors and students from Idaho State University. All of them added to the interesting and diverse speakeasy sub-subculture. The pimps, hustlers, and prostitutes from Seattle also caught my attention.

I never saw any other kids when I was with my dad at the speakeasies. I felt special because everyone acknowledged me, gave me money, and bought me sodas and candy bars. Besides the soda and candy, my father allowed me to take sips of his beer. Sometimes, I just helped myself to my father's beer when the environment was busy, but I made sure I never got in the way. I went with my dad to several speakeasies several times a week, and sometimes, we visited multiple establishments on the same day. I especially liked going to May Collins's place when my dad played cards. May was kind to me. She hugged and kissed me and let me stay in her private living quarters to watch TV. When she left to take care of business, I would sneak into the refrigerator and take sips of whatever alcohol was available. I'd also sneak over to a cabinet where she stored a variety of booze and sneak sips. I mainly looked for gin or vodka since they were the most odorless. One time, she left the storage room unlocked. I peeked inside and saw boxes full of bottles of booze, bags of weed and drugs, and stacks of money on some of the shelves.

My Mom Washing in the Word

When we moved from the dungeon to the projects, my mother started reading the bible more often. She fully understood the spiritual war that confronted her and said that the only weapon against it was the supernatural power in God's Word. My brother and I attended her devotional studies more often than our sister. Plus, our mom seemed to direct her attention more to me than my brother. My sister and brother were more studious and engaged in more wholesome activities. I believe Mom focused more on me because my personality was very different from those of my siblings. I tended to drift on a different course and stretched our mother's limits, which led to her concern about my behavior.

As I mentioned earlier, we often read from the Psalms and Proverbs, and Mom emphasized the importance of remembering Psalm 23 and Proverbs 23. The latter warned of the dangers of alcoholism. I believe my mother used reading the Proverbs to counter my habit of hanging out with my dad at the speakeasies. Looking back, I see that my mother's concerns about the time I spent at speakeasies with my father were well-founded. By the time I was ten, I was a full-fledged alcoholic and had learned how to hide it.

My mother repeatedly paraphrased one of her bible verses, like John 8:12: "If you walk in darkness, you can't see where you're going." She warned me about keeping bad company. My mother's little saying was paramount about the development of my Dr. Jekyll and Mr. Hyde dueling personalities when I was young. I was deceiving myself about drinking, knowing my mother would be horribly upset if she knew how much I was drinking.

Dr. Jekyll, the kind and respectful me, dwelled in my soul during normal behavior with my mother. The deceitful Mr. Hyde infiltrated my mind and soul when I was away from my mother. A carefree speakeasy mentality would overcome me, and any discernment between right and wrong escaped me while being chased with a desire to drink alcohol.

The speakeasies were busy and exciting places. They were environments where several of the old Black guys used colorful language, except for my dad. The profanity would go to a more humorous level when the speakeasy owner played comedy records of Red Foxx, Rudy Ray Moore, and other Black comedians as my dad and the other men continued to talk and laugh. Tiny, May Collins, and Pete Morgan would frequently give my dad complimentary drinks to show their appreciation, and I would frequently help myself when possible.

When my dad showed up, some folks tended to linger a little longer and spend more money. I would usually sit in an out-of-the-way spot but kept track of my dad and his drinks. I would take advantage of the dynamically busy environment and sneak a drink of my dad's cold beer or take a sip from his shot glass of liquor when possible. I liked the burning rush that slowly propelled my mind into a state of limbo.

Much later in life, I had to terms with the abnormal conditioning I had been exposed to since about the age of five. My Mr. Hyde was undergoing some seriously disturbing development, plus I was slowly being conditioned into an early life of alcoholism. I believe the alcoholic conditioning left me unaware of when the transformation between the two conflicting personalities occurred. The transformation was automatic, and yet everything appeared normal to me.

I believe that throughout my early years, my mother sensed something more was going on with me, and she set out to establish a broader biblical foundation for me. I believe she saw that her baby son needed more help compared to my siblings. At such a young age, I was influenced by a darkness that became my norm. I was much like a leaf caught up in a storm run-off, drifting toward the ocean.

CHAPTER

4

STARTING SCHOOL AND ESCAPING THE TRIANGLE

The First Day at Bonneville

Pocatello was still plagued by discrimination and segregation in 1956 when I started attending Bonneville Elementary School. My first day was a little intimidating because so many bigger and older kids surrounded me. The most memorable thing about my first day occurred at the end of the day. I made my exit from the schoolhouse and walked across the large playing area. I looked, and on the corner of 6th and Lander sat my faithful companion, our beautiful golden cocker spaniel retriever named Tuffy.

Once I started school, I had more freedom to expand my boundaries and explore more of the town. Despite the discrimination and segregation, I don't recall experiencing any racial issues in elementary school or from any of the businesses in Pocatello. However, Black adults faced a variety of race issues.

My first racial incident occurred when I went home with a White girl schoolmate. We walked into her house, and she turned to me and told me to wait in the living room as she called out to her mom. Her mom walked through a doorway while drying her hands with a towel. She looked up, saw me, and stopped dead in her tracks. Her jaw dropped in total shock, and she turned white as a ghost. She gestured to her daughter to come to her and told me, "Just a moment, please." They disappeared through the doorway where the mom had come from. I could hear them talking as they continued further into the house, and then there was silence.

In a few moments, the girl's dad walked into the living room. He calmly walked past me, opened the front door and the screen door, stepped out, and said, "It's time for you to go." So, I left.

I walked away, not knowing what to think. At first, I was deeply saddened by the incident, but I wasn't angry; I felt *empty*. Then, I remembered my mother warning me that there would be times when I would not be accepted, and I couldn't let it keep me down. She emphasized that people who don't have the heart of Jesus will always have racial issues, and we must pray for them and look past them.

Though I was confused as I walked away from my friend's house that day, I thought about what my mom said, and the emptiness and sorrow started to drift away.

Father Fighting for Life

Early one morning, I was awakened by some noise. I got up and walked down the hallway to the kitchen. My father and mother were engaged in a fight—a real deadly battle. My father was trying to wrestle a large butcher knife from my mother and was bleeding from a cut on the side of his face and his shoulder. When they noticed us children watching, they stopped fighting, and we all stood looking at each other.

A day later, my mother, sister, brother, and I were on a train leaving Pocatello. I asked my brother where we were going, and he said we were going to our grandmother's house in Little Rock, Arkansas. It took about three days to get to Little Rock. Since our dad worked for Union Pacific Railroad, we could travel for free on the Union Pacific line and half-fare on other lines. I knew several Union Pacific porters and waiters from seeing them around Pocatello and at the speakeasies. When the train made its scheduled stops, I was allowed to stand on the platform between the train cars and watch the train workers loading and unloading cargo and passengers.

We finally arrived in Little Rock, where my uncle picked us up at the train station. We had a distance to drive because my grandmother lived on the outskirts of Little Rock. Being in this strange, hot, muggy place was very different, but it didn't take long for me to acclimate and make myself right at home.

My grandmother resembled the smiling granny on Aunt Jemima syrup bottles. She wore the same scarf and dress with a similar print and an apron. The apron was spotted with light brown stains from the tobacco she chewed. My grandmother was a nice-looking, light-brown-skinned Southern woman and extremely mobile and agile.

Where she lived was beautiful and peaceful, yet dangerous, so there were boundaries set for me not to go far from the house. I soon suffered the consequences of not honoring the boundaries. One day, I decided to stretch out, but I got caught. In my grandmother's calm, slow, Southern way, I could tell she was upset with me. She reminded me of that fact by saying, "A hard head ends up with a soft behind," which was her way of saying I was going to get my butt beat.

As she walked toward me, my grandmother slowly lumbered over to a tree and broke off a good-sized limb, all while describing my fate in detail. I didn't think she was going to put too much of a hurting on me, but she raised her thick arm and brought that limb down on my rear end. It hurt like crazy. Before I could recover from the first blow, she quickly grabbed me and swiftly delivered blow after blow, hard and continually.

Pretty soon, I was on the ground, squirming like a snail doused with salt. I called out to my mother, but the look on my mom's face told me she wanted nothing to do with what I was getting for fear she'd be next. She backed off and left me to my grandmother, beating my tail. After my whipping was over, my grandmother went into the house.

Soon, my grandmother called me into the house and talked to me in a calm, soothing voice. She said something about riding the evil out of a hard-headed little boy. Much later in life, when I thought about the beating, I wondered if she was talking about Proverbs 23:13–14: "[13]Do not withhold correction from a child, For if you beat him with a rod, he will not die. [14]You shall beat him with a rod And deliver his soul from hell", and probably so.

My mom took my brother and sister out of school when we left Pocatello and enrolled them in school shortly after arriving in Little Rock. I was pre-school age, so I didn't go to school. About six weeks later, we headed back to the train station, boarded a train, and returned to Pocatello. Despite the short time we were in Little Rock, I have some fond memories of the place.

One Sunday, my drunk uncle was outside chasing a chicken to butcher and dress for dinner. He caught the chicken with his left hand and swung it around and around in the air, wringing its neck. Then he plopped the chicken down on a tree stump, swung a small axe in his right hand, and chopped off the chicken's head.

The chicken flopped off the tree stump and hit the ground. It fluttered around on the ground, then it got on its feet and started running around the yard without a head. Blood was squirting everywhere from its neck. Then, the chicken suddenly took off flying. It was amazing to watch it fly around and around in the air without a head! Then, the headless bird let out a stream of poop as it flew.

Everyone took off running for cover, trying to avoid the swirling chicken poop. My grandmother's house was built on stilts about four feet off the ground as a precaution against periodic flooding, so I dove under one side of the house. Unfortunately, I ended up near a goose nest. I saw the mother goose running toward me from the other side of the house, squawking like crazy. I quickly backed out from underneath the house and ran, somehow managing to avoid the flying chicken poop.

When we returned to Pocatello, whatever the issue had been between our mother and father appeared to be settled. Still, I had no idea why they had been fighting, so I asked my brother. He didn't know either. For some time, I wondered why our parents were fighting. It was disturbing for a while, but I soon got over it as I continued to accompany my father to the speakeasies.

The remainder of my elementary years were all about me venturing out more in Pocatello. As I grew older and got promoted to higher grades, I was allowed to go across town by myself, which was a big deal. Normally, I would go across town with my mother or father to shop, visit a great ice cream parlor, or watch a Sunday movie at the Chief Theater with my sister, brother, and friends. The ability to go anywhere in Pocatello was a great joy for me. I could go to any store and never encounter any racial issues. Sometimes, I would even take a White girl schoolmate to a drug store and treat her to a root beer, cream soda, or orange cream soda, or we would share a banana split or sundae. We encountered no issues.

My mother cultivated confidence in me, so I wasn't afraid to go about Pocatello on my own. She kept things simple. Time and time again, she told me that it was about the heart. And people who didn't have the heart of Jesus could only do what was immediately on their minds. My mom was always right about things that popped up in my life. I knew I should always do what my mom said, but I constantly struggled with doing the right thing.

A continuously growing battle waged in my mind and soul with the conflict between indwelling Dr. Jekyll and Mr. Hyde. When I was with my mother, the respectful Dr. Jekyll influenced me to do the right thing. But when I was away from my mother, my evil Mr. Hyde bullied and intimidated Dr. Jekyll into quiet submission. I was young, and it was so complicated for me to decide whether to do the right thing.

Whenever I did something undesirable, my decision was sealed by the approval of an immature, flawed conscience. My conscience was under the sway of Mr. Hyde's self-centered, self-preserving nature, leaving little room to reason about doing the right thing. Plus, Mr. Hyde's devious character was shaped and nurtured in the speakeasy training ground. It was a carefree environment influenced by hipsters, hustlers, and older Black guys with their swagger and slang. I didn't understand how all this would affect me down the road, but my mother did.

From 4th Street to 9th Street

One day, I overheard my parents talking about moving to 9th Street. On 9th Street, all the sidewalks were intact. The houses had nice front yards and big backyards with green lawns. Most of the houses on the block had four bedrooms, nice kitchens, dining and living areas, and full basements. Ninth Street was quiet, with very little traffic, and safe for neighborhood kids.

Our new house was different from the other houses on the block. It was a little more than a multi-room shack. My brother and I still had to share a bedroom with our dad, and my mother and sister continued to share a room. But we had a nice front and back yard.

One day at school, I heard an announcement that Bonneville Elementary was closing, and all students would attend different elementary schools, depending on school district boundaries. I was sent to Roosevelt Elementary School in the Alameda area along with two other Black girls in my class. We were the first Black students to attend the school.

On the first day at Roosevelt, the school day came to an end, and outside beside the school, two White boys confronted me. One of the boys walked toward me and said, "Hey, n****r!" I didn't say a word, but before anyone said anything else, I punched the kid in the face, and he went down.

The other kid took off running, but I chased him, tackled him to the ground, turned him over, sat on his chest, and slammed a couple of punches in his face. I got up off the kid, who had blood running from his mouth and nose.

I went around the building and started walking down the street toward home. I saw my two Black girl schoolmates walking, so I ran and caught up with them. They didn't know about my incident with the two boys. I didn't give it a second thought, nor did I mention it to my mom or dad when I got home.

The next day, the girls and I arrived at school, and two familiar White boys came running up to me and greeted me with great excitement. I recognized them from playing against them in recreational sports in Pocatello. A small crowd of kids followed them and watched us as we talked and laughed. Later that day, several other boys came up to me to say hello. Some of them I recognized, and some I didn't, but they all recognized me. I experienced no more racial issues or incidents for the remainder of the school year at Roosevelt.

I was sad about finishing sixth grade. I was also extremely excited because I was headed for Franklin Junior High School. Franklin was a major step for me. It was one step closer to Pocatello Senior High School. Getting to Poky High had always been one of my major goals.

CHAPTER

5

FUN-FILLED JUNIOR HIGH SCHOOL YEARS

First Year—Franklin Junior High School

Before long, I left Roosevelt Elementary School and entered Franklin Junior High School. My trek through elementary school had been about learning how to flap my wings, and junior high school was about taking flight. Attending Franklin Junior High School was the beginning of a rite of passage to my grand entry into Pocatello High School. I knew the high school fight song before I knew the Franklin Junior High fight song!

At Franklin, I was immediately confronted with a huge legacy issue left by my sister and my brother. My sister was three years older, and my brother was two years older. Both were scholars and overachievers. Then there was me. It was a tall order to be constantly compared to them, so I had to cut my path through school with sports leading the way.

It was especially challenging to compete with my brother's legacy. I'm talking about someone who wrote musical arrangements in junior high school. His primary musical instruments were the piano and the flute, but he could play many instruments in the woodwind family, including keyboards and percussion. My mother started my brother with piano lessons between six and seven; he was a natural. He excelled with Mr. Gowns, the piano teacher. I also took lessons for a while, but they abruptly ended when my mother discovered that I was skipping lessons and embezzling the funds. When my mom found out I was lying to her, I received a severe beating. I have always been amazed that my brother didn't tell on me.

Franklin Junior High School was fun because I already knew several students. I don't recall any racial issues with any of my White classmates, but I had encounters with a couple of dads. There were two girls I would occasionally meet up with, and we would walk to school. A couple of weeks into school, I was walking home one day, and a truck pulled up to the curb. A White man leaned out of the driver's window and said to me, "Hey, boy, don't get any ideas with my daughter," and then he drove away. I was more angry than frightened. My first thought was to find this guy's truck and set it on fire. I found it interesting how quickly my mind drifted toward revenge.

A week or so later, I was again walking home after school with a White boy schoolmate when a car pulled over to the curb. A different White guy leaned out of the driver's window and said, "I don't want you hanging around my daughter, so you better stay away from her," and then he drove away. The nerve of this guy thinking that I should be afraid of him! There I was again, steaming mad with revenge on my mind.

Both times, my saving grace was remembering what my mom said. She reminded me that things like the two dads were going to happen with people who, again, lacked the love of Jesus in their hearts. I eventually dropped the anger for both dads and moved on. I continued walking with both the girls whenever I met them on the way to school despite their dads, and I never told the girls.

Sports was my way of establishing myself. We engaged in a variety of sports for physical education (PE) class, but Franklin also had organized sports like contact football, basketball, wrestling, and track. Football was in full swing when school started, so I asked my mom if I could try out for football. She said yes, so I went and didn't make the cut. I was devastated when some of my White friends made the cut, and I cried uncontrollably walking on the way home. Before I reached our house, I stopped crying and cleaned myself up. When I entered the house, my mother knew something was up and asked me what was wrong. I told her and started crying again. My mom hugged me and told me not to cry, to be patient, and maybe something would change down the road, and I'd get another chance. It was something to pray about.

A week passed when a coach approached me one day during PE and told me that if I still wanted to play football, I should go to the equipment room and check out some gear. I ran to the equipment room to collect a uniform, put it in my wall locker, and returned to class. When school was over, I ran to the dressing room, put my uniform on, and took off to the practice field. The coach approached me at the end of practice and told me, "Good practice," so I made the Franklin Junior High School junior varsity football team and was the happiest kid in the world.

Second Year—Franklin Junior High School

I was looking forward to going into my second year at Franklin. The first year was about finding my way through the unknown. In the second year, I was so much more confident. I also met a different crowd of White guys who were not jocks. These guys smoked, stole beer from stores, and stirred up the troublesome Mr. Hyde lurking within me.

School became a breeze because I played sports, and my buddy John gave me the nickname, Jocko. As I stated earlier, I was not as studious as my sister or brother, but I maintained average grades to qualify for sports. I had a great time during my first two years at Franklin, and I started to be viewed and treated differently by my classmates and some teachers, putting some distance between my sister's and my brother's legacy.

Third Year—Franklin Junior High School

By my third year at Franklin, I was engaged in several mischievous things with some troubled boys. Things like placing a carton of rotten milk in the school's heating vents and pulling the fire alarm (both good for getting out of class early), putting Super Glue on door latches to keep classrooms closed, placing tacks on classroom seats, and dropping cherry bombs into toilets.

A male PE teacher and sports coach was also a real pain in a most private place, so he became a favorite target. A tack in his seat or gluing his grading book to his desk was always a good laugh. He would get so upset that he would eventually tear the book to shreds. We would carefully break several of his wooden pencils and put them back together, and the class roared in laughter when he tried to use them. Placing a jack-in-the-box gag in his desk drawer, and the class roared again when he opened the drawer. Food coloring in his Thermos was a big laugh. And when he defiantly parked his car on our outdoor basketball court outside the dressing room, we put a couple of large garbage cans in the backseat of his car. Once, I snuck into the coach's dressing room and loaded his shoes with Vaseline.

One other time, on a dare before our PE class started, I lined his jock strap with an injury repair ointment called Atomic Balm. The class ran down to Caldwell Park for PE that day to play soccer. When we arrived at the park, the class stood in formation for attendance. The coach started calling roll, and soon after, he started to twitch and squirm. Then, he suddenly dropped his clipboard and took off running back to the school, and the whole class roared with laughter.

It probably sounds like junior high school was a carnival. It was a lot of fun, but I also learned and developed a strong respect for good teachers, and I truly enjoyed school and learning. Unfortunately, a few of my teachers continued to expect me to perform at the academic level of my sister and brother, but that was never going to happen.

I experienced a very interesting incident with a White girl classmate and her dad. This girl was a giddy troublemaker but in a fun way. One day, she asked me, "Would you like to go to my house after school to help me give my dad a little surprise?" I was puzzled, so I asked her what she wanted. She told me that her dad was too serious, and she wanted to loosen him up. She had already set her dad up by telling him that she was going to date and probably marry a Black man.

After she explained her plan, I looked at her and laughed. "Okay." With my slanted sense of humor, I could picture her dad's face, and I thought it would be interesting and funny. Her dad and I were familiar with each other because he came to our basketball and football games.

The time arrived so we went to her big house after school. She opened the front door, and we entered a spacious living room. Her mother warmly greeted me, and soon after, her father joined us and also warmly greeted me. I hung out with her for about forty-five minutes, and then I decided to leave.

I walked out the front door and headed down the walkway to the gate. Suddenly, her father came rushing from around the side of the house, and he called me. He was calm and non-threatening as he approached and asked me, "Excuse me, Presley, but are you dating my daughter?"

He had the strangest look on his face. It was a look of desperation, like he was hoping I would say no. I could tell he was truly worried but not angry. I wanted to tell him no, but at the same time, I didn't want to ruin his daughter's little setup, and Mr. Hyde was tapping me on the shoulder, encouraging me to play the game.

I looked at him and smiled, and I didn't say a word as I turned around and walked away. I walked through the gate and started walking down the sidewalk. I got a little down the sidewalk and looked back over my shoulder. He was still standing in the yard, watching me walk away. I started feeling a little guilty about the whole charade. I knew what I was doing was wrong, and my mother would be terribly upset about me being so deceitful, but it was still exciting at the same time. I figured that over time, the dad would be able to see that his daughter and I were not hooking up. The girl and I remained close friends and spent time together, but we never romantically dated.

CHAPTER
6

MY FATHER DIED

On November 18, 1965, I was home. At around 7:45 p.m. a doctor at the hospital in Rupert, Idaho, called and told me my father died. My mother was next door visiting the Woods, so I completed the call with the doctor, hung up the phone, put on a coat, and walked next door. I knocked on their door, and Mr. Woods answered. He invited me in and told me my mother was in the kitchen with Mrs. Woods, so I followed Mr. Woods into the kitchen. I looked at my mother and said to her, "Mom, the doctor called and said my daddy died." Mrs. Woods screamed, burst into tears, jumped out of her chair, and started beating her chest.

My mother didn't say a word. She calmly stood up from her chair, walked to the living room, put her coat on, walked out the door, and we went home. When we arrived home, she called the doctor. She talked to him for a while and hung up. She then called my sister, Mildred, in Kansas City, Missouri (my father's first daughter from a previous marriage), followed by calls to several other people. Within an hour, our little house was full of people, and everyone greeted me and hugged me. After a while, I put on my coat and went out the back door. I stood on the back porch staring at the sky and wondered why I hadn't cried yet.

After moving to 9th Street, our house became a little spruced-up shack, still with a nice front yard and a beautiful spacious green back lawn. My dad loved working in the yard with its perfectly trimmed edges. He used to make my brother and me get up early on Saturday mornings to help manicure the yard. I hated getting up on those early Saturday mornings, but suddenly, standing there, my heart was heavy with regret.

Days after my father's death and a few days after Thanksgiving vacation, my sister, brother, and I were back in school. I was looking forward to returning to school because Coach White, our basketball coach, was a great guy. He was truly inspiring in how he treated us players, and I especially wanted to be with him. The ninth-grade White guys I played with at Franklin Junior High were also great, and the coach taught us a basketball system called "The Wyoming Weave." Our team was smart and fast, and we picked up the "weave" and ran it with high efficiency, destroying the other junior high school teams. This was all I wanted to think about and all I wanted to do and not think about my father's death.

Naturally, word got out, and several of my teammates and classmates attended my father's funeral. My mother arranged the funeral, and I recall her being extremely busy, being driven around town by Mr. Woods, Mr. Stokes, and several other folks.

I don't recall what happened to my father's 1947 Desoto. My father's old car was in immaculate shape and running condition. He cared for his old car like it was a brand-new Cadillac. The only blemish on the car was on a side panel that my dad repaired after I side-swiped a car early one morning when I snuck the car away for joyriding.

I used to go everywhere with my dad. When I was smaller, he would drive, sit me in his lap, and help me steer as he worked the pedals. As I got bigger, he would let me drive on my own. We would drive the back roads of Pocatello while he drank a can of Olympia Beer and hunted for grouse and doves with a 410 shotgun he kept in the trunk of the car.

I don't know what happened to my father's car. I think my mother sold it to wash away tainted memories, but I could have driven her around if she had kept it.

I was living in a perpetual state of shock. When my mind was at rest, all I would think about were the times I spent with my dad. I even thought about the time when he almost killed my brother.

We had finished pheasant hunting and were getting ready to head back home. My brother had cleared his shotgun, placed it in the car's trunk, opened the back door, and sat behind the driver's seat. My father was clearing the bolt action on the 410 shotgun, and sometimes the bolt would stick. In his effort to clear it, he would hit the bolt with the butt of his hand, but he was unaware that he was raising the gun barrel as he hit the bolt. He gave the bolt one last good strike, the bolt slide finally seated, and the gun fired off. The gun blast went through the open back passenger door, across my brother's chest, and out the other side of the car. My father became a total wreck, and it took a long time for him to recover before he was able to drive us home.

I remember back when we had been on 9th Street for a couple of years when one Sunday morning, my father and brother got into a fight, and my dad pistol-whipped my brother. We were outside, getting ready to get in the car to go to church. My brother didn't want to go, and my father and brother started to argue. My dad grabbed my brother, and they started to wrestle and fight. Soon, my brother was on the ground, and my father was on top of him. Then, out of nowhere, a pistol appeared in my father's hand. My father started hitting my brother upside his head as I stood watching in total shock. Pretty soon, Mr. Stokes and Mr. Woods were outside, grabbing my father and pulling him off my brother. Mr. Woods took the gun from my father as Mr. Stokes helped my brother.

My sister and brother were always at odds with our father, and I could never understand why they were always in contention with him. As I grew older, I began to reason within myself that the fundamental problem was that my father, sister, and brother were too much alike. As time passed, I would think that my father should have been more than a basic provider in a family with such intelligent and aggressive children as my sister and brother.

Suddenly, a terrible thought hit me. I could no longer run around Pocatello with my dad to pick up a broken TV or deliver a fixed one. I would no longer be able to go with him to someone's house or farm to help fix a vehicle or something. I would no longer be hanging out with my dad at the speakeasies.

I would forever miss walking into a speakeasy with my dad and having one of the men shout out, "Hey, Vann! What's the deal!" Dad would respond with something like, "Man, if I knew what the deal is, I would go get it and spread it around!" Then they all would laugh. Then someone else would say something like, "Hey, Vann, what would ol' Nat be singing today?" And my dad would start off singing "Mona Lisa" by Nat King Cole, and he would sound almost like him. Then he would mix in a little whistling that sounded even more like Nat, and I would beam with pride.

In 1958, my father enrolled in the DeVry home correspondence electronics course, and the math and science from his previous machinist and welding training prepared him to learn electronics. I recall getting up early some mornings and cranking the handle on an 8mm projector he used with his lessons. I can still see a cartoon character flashing against the wall as he learned the elements of Ohm's Law.

My father built his test equipment from Heath Kits, and he performed the soldering for the kits because of his welding experience. Our first TV was a black-and-white unit that he picked up and repaired. My father got pretty good at fixing radios and black-and-white TVs for folks all over town, and he was in the process of starting a small business. When he started troubleshooting color TVs, it was very different from fixing black-and-white TVs, and he was so excited to learn, but he died as he was starting to make headway into color TVs.

My older sister Mildred lived in Kansas City, Missouri. She was my father's daughter from a previous marriage. My father was born in 1902, my mother was born in 1912, and my sister Mildred was only nine years younger than my mother. I remember talking to Mildred about our dad and his thirst for learning. One time, she told me in her slow, Midwestern drawl, "Ya honey, your daddy came off that reservation and went to them government schools, and he became all this, and he thought he was all that!" My sister Mildred told me that my dad spent his early childhood on an Indian reservation and later moved to a plot of land provided by government land grants, and that's when he began to excel with his education.

Being with my dad at the speakeasies, I could see he was someone special, and he later proved it to me by completing the DeVry home correspondence electronics course. My dad was a perfect example of how education can work for someone.

Thanksgiving had come and gone, and it only meant something because of my mom's great Thanksgiving dinner with turkey, her cornbread dressing with silky giblet gravy, collard greens, her wonderful sweet potato casserole, cranberry sauce, and all of it topped off with her famous yeast rolls. Christmas was a "don't care" for me, along with the coming New Year. My sixteenth birthday rolled around, and I couldn't have cared less about anything.

Finally, a bright light. Mrs. Idaho Purse hooked me up with a great summer job working in the labor pool at the Nation Reactor Testing Station in the Arco Desert. The job required a bus trip, leaving at 6 a.m. and returning to Pocatello at 6 p.m. The job was a great distraction with early traveling hours and great pay, and I loved it. But my dad was dead and gone, and I missed him in the worst way. The strange thing was that neither my mother nor I had shed a tear yet, and I felt that my mom and tears were all I had to look forward to.

7

DARKNESS BLOOMING IN HIGH SCHOOL

Before Starting High School

A lot was going on starting my sophomore year. I was working a great summer job, preparing to start my first year of high school, and we were staying at the Bethel Baptist Church parsonage during the 9th Street house renovation. J. D. Harris was opposed to my mom staying in the church parsonage. He was opposed to her staying because my mother's voice was one of the loudest, exposing his hypocrisy. J. D. Harris was supposed to be an ordained Baptist minister, but he also basked in his iniquity of bootlegging, loansharking, and occasional pimping.

Despite his protest, the church elders and deacons allowed my mom to rent the parsonage, and I started to plot my revenge against the old cuss for stressing my mother out. Later, with the house renovation completed, we moved back to 9th Street. My mom allowed me to buy a grand, old, classic four-door 1955 Chevrolet Bel Air Sedan with only 14,000 miles, AM/FM Radio, leather seats, with interior wood trim for $200. My new car helped me not to dwell on J. D. Harris's revenge.

My busy summer was ending, along with my job at the National Reactor Testing Station, normally called the Site. I owe it all to Mrs. Idaho Purse for setting me up with my first real job along with her work ethic tutoring. It had been a couple of years since the Civil Rights Act of 1964 passed, but Mrs. Purse talked to me about respecting and protecting hard-earned employment opportunities.

Soon after we returned to the remodeled 9th Street house, my mother started seeing a guy named Mr. Robertson, who was a popular skilled mason. He offered me a job one day, and I agreed to work for him as a hod carrier. I worked from 6 a.m. to 6 p.m. the whole week and did a final cleanup last Saturday. I received only $135 for working five twelve-hour days and a miserable Saturday morning cleanup time. I felt cheated, and revenge was all I could think about.

My life changed dramatically with my new car. I started visiting a couple of stores where some of my schoolmates worked. They would sneak a case of beer and put it in a pre-determined location. I would drive to the store, pick up the beer, put it on ice in the trunk of my car, meet them after work, and we would hang out and drink.

One day, as I was driving down Lander Street, I pulled over and went to Tiny's speakeasy. I knocked on the door and Tiny answered the door and screamed. She reached out, wrapped me in her arms, picked me up off the ground, and carried me inside with her 6", 200 lbs. frame. There were several elderly Black men in the room who got up to greet me with handshakes, pats on the back, and kind words of condolences for the loss of my father.

Tiny wiped the tears from her eyes and asked me if I wanted a drink. I replied yes. It felt like I was there with my father. She started talking about how much she missed my dad and what a great man he was. All the other men chimed in with sincere appreciation. I was at Tiny's for a couple of hours. I consumed three shots with beer chasers and didn't spend a dime.

When I left Tiny's, I began to wonder about the other speakeasies and whether I would be greeted warmly. I would have to find out some other day because I was pretty fired up from what I put away. I probably shouldn't have been driving, but in my mind, I was doing fine. Little did I realize that this was the start of a whole new level of hard-core drinking.

First Day at Pocatello High School

My first day of high school started badly. I was excited about presenting my best, so I dressed in my favorite Temptations outfit: a light brown vest and slacks with a gold French-cuffed shirt with gold cuff links, sporting a gold tie, and topped with a pair of tan suede shoes. I got a lot of looks and smiles from several girls, which was my goal.

I walked into my first class. All the seats were taken, so I had to stand in the back with a group of students. The female teacher was taking attendance and soon reached the end of her list. She picked up a clipboard for the student names standing in the back of the room, looked straight at me, and said, "What's your name, Sunshine?"

I immediately saw red. "My name is not Sunshine, you fat b***h."

The room fell instantly silent except for a few chuckles. She was stunned, turned beet red, and said, "That kind of language is unnecessary and tolerated here."

"No, what's unnecessary is for a big-mouth heifer like you not asking my name!"

Then she said, "Please leave my classroom and report to the principal's office."

I replied, "Gladly, you fat b***h!"

I made my way to the principal's office. The secretary asked if she could help me, and I said, "Yes, some teacher was calling me racial names, and I cussed her out, and she kicked me out of class."

The principal heard me talking, and he came out of his office and motioned me to his office. "We don't curse at teachers, so what's going on?"

As he sat down, I said, "The teacher didn't know my name, and I did not like the racial slur being called 'Sunshine.' I let her know about it, so she will get respect when she gives respect."

He asked who the teacher was, and I told him I didn't know her name. He said to sit in the hall until the bell rang for my next class, and he would get back to me.

Before the end of my last class, a student entered the classroom and gave the teacher a note. The teacher read the note out loud: "Presley Vann, please report to the principal's office at the end of class."

I made my way to the principal's office. I opened the office door and walked in, and the secretary said, "Go right in. They're waiting for you."

When I walked in, the teacher I cursed at was there. She turned to me and said, "I am sorry if I insulted you. That was not my intent." I'm sure I surprised them when I returned a sincere apology.

Then I heard it. "So, you're Alfred's brother?" The teacher proceeded to tell me what a wonderful student my brother was and how he was still a joy to talk to since he was a senior at the time. She said, "I look forward to having you in my class."

I shook her hand. "Thank you, and I am sorry for the language. I'm looking forward to attending your class."

The teacher left, and the principal said, "Alfred is a great student. I look forward to you joining us. I understand you're playing football; you better get to practice."

I replied, "Yes, sir, and again, I'm sorry." Again, my response impressed him as I left his office. I thought, *Wow! There it was. Because of my brother, another bad situation turned good.* I would hear it again from a couple of other teachers about how wonderful my brother was, but I wouldn't get it rammed down my throat like at Franklin Junior High. I made it through Thanksgiving, Christmas, New Year's, and now the end of my first year in high school. I found myself missing my father even more, and the confusion about my mourning him continued to mount. Excessive drinking became a natural thing for me, and I was doing a good job of hiding it. Fortunately, my mom worked a lot, so concealing it from her was easy. A few times, I slipped around her when she knew I was either drunk or high. I unconditionally loved my mother. She was always there for us, especially my brother and me, his music and my sports. So, my guilt would painfully throb after being drunk or high around her.

I missed my dad so much that school was becoming less of a priority, and I began to feel like I didn't want to go anymore. Things were beginning to weigh on me, but so many people encouraged me to stay in school—several older Black guys like Frank King, Mr. Stokes, Mr. Woods, my old buddy Heyward Evans, and even Logan Thomas, Senior, and my older nephew Robbie, my favorite drinking buddy Darwin, and several folks at the speakeasies.

Even though Darwin was older than my sister, we became tight friends, even to where he would supply me with the booze I took to my neighborhood parties. Darwin was a real character. It seemed like if I was not at home, in school, playing sports, or with my buddy Daniel, I was with Darwin, cruising around partying in his 1964 Chevy Nova SS. Darwin and I would sometimes buy and split a roasted chicken and a huge Texas donut and wash them down with a small chocolate milk. Sometimes, after midnight, we would go to the old Pocatello cemetery, share a joint, drink shots with wine cooler chasers, and look for strange lights and activity in the night.

There's a popular song, "For What It's Worth" by Buffalo Springfield, and in the song is a line that sums up my mental state at the time: "There's something happening here. What it is ain't exactly clear." I didn't want to be in Pocatello anymore, but I had nowhere else to go. I didn't want to go to school anymore, but I couldn't quit. There wasn't anything wrong, yet everything was wrong, and I depressingly missed my dad.

Junior Year at Poky High

My seventeenth birthday rolled around, and it didn't mean much to me. My brother moved out of our mother's house, and missing my dad was becoming a burden. The last day of school arrived, and my Black buddy Daniel and I were at my mom's house, drinking wine coolers and listening to "MacArthur Park" by Richard Harris. I decided to visit a White girl I met in my sophomore year.

We were soon riding down an alley a block from the high school. I was creeping slowly down the alley because she warned me about her father, who wanted her to have nothing to do with Black guys. We met briefly in the alley behind her house, and suddenly, her dad started driving up the alley, so Daniel and I took off.

We decided to drive over to a gas station tended by a druggy buddy I called Teddy. We arrived at the station and parked in the back. We got out of the car and walked through the side entrance. Teddy, Larry, and Thane were drinking beer and passing a joint. They were on their way to being well done while listening to "Sunshine of Your

Love" by Cream. Daniel and I joined in, and we offered up the beer in the trunk of my car, so Daniel took off to get the beer.

As soon as Daniel returned with the beer, a lady came racing into the station lot and stopped her truck at a far pump. She jumped out of the truck and started running across the station bay area, shouting, "Please! Please, you have to help my dad. I think he had a heart attack." Everybody was extremely high except for Daniel and me.

I looked at Teddy, and he gave me an empty, blank stare. I ran out to the truck's driver's side door, which she had left open. I looked in the truck, and I could see her father slumped over in the passenger seat. There was not enough room for her to ride with me, so I yelled back to the group to have someone drive her to St. Anthony Hospital. I jumped in behind the wheel, closed the door, and made my way to St. Anthony Hospital Emergency.

As I was driving, I noticed the old dude was more than just slumped over in the seat; his body had weirdly collapsed, hanging over the edge like a big blob. I could sense a strange stillness about the old guy. I could tell he was truly dead. My heart sank, and I felt sorry for him, but it was still a little creepy being in the truck with his massive, lifeless form.

I eventually pulled into the hospital emergency driveway. I slammed on the brakes and parked at the entrance. I jumped out of the truck and ran into the emergency room, yelling, "There's a man outside with a heart attack, and I think he's dead!"

Several ER workers jumped up and rushed to the truck, pushing a gurney as I followed. One aid opened the passenger door, and two other aids started tugging and pulling on the big guy, trying to get the huge guy out of the truck.

They finally got his shoulders out the truck door, followed by his hips, and then his huge limp body poured out like a giant slug slithering down a flight of stairs. He fell out of the truck and hit the ground. The aids were struggling to pick him up and put him on the gurney, so I rushed over and joined in the struggle. After what seemed like an eternity, we got him on the gurney and wheeled him through the emergency door.

The truck was still running, so I jumped back behind the wheel and parked it in a guest parking spot. I turned off the truck, walked back into the ER, and gave the keys to a nurse. My mother was on duty as a nurse's aide. I saw her enter the ER as a doctor approached me and started asking questions. I finished answering the doctor's questions and then turned and walked out the door to wait for someone to drive up with the poor guy's daughter.

The emergency door opened, and my mom stepped outside and called out to me, "Hey, are you all right?"

"Yes, I'm okay," I replied.

"Well, it looks like you got him here in the nick of time; they were able to get his heart beating again." Then Mom turned and went back inside as I walked to the corner.

I stood on the corner feeling a little strange. I noticed my shirt and pants were clinging to my body and wondered what the heck was going on. Then, I figured it out. When the old guy was dying in the truck, his bowels relaxed, and he peed and pooped on the truck bench seat. My pants, shirt, underwear, and socks were soaked with the dead man's run-off. I freaked out and started screaming and stripping right there on the street corner. I stood there, stark naked as the day I was born. It was horrible! I started creeping down the street, completely nude. Fortunately, my mom's house was not that far away. We lived near 9th and Sherman, and I was currently on 8th and Bridger, so I took off running down 8th Street towards my mom's house.

I came to a yard that had a sprinkler on. I opened the gate and stood in the middle of the sprinkler to wash off as best I could. The house's front door was open, and a lady stepped onto her porch. I took off running back down 8th Street, wondering what was going through the lady's mind. I was soon turning and running up the alley on Sherman. I made it to the gate, opened it, and raced across the backyard of my mom's house. I ran up to a locked back door to which I had no key. My house key and wallet were still in my cadaver fluid-soaked pants at the corner of the hospital parking lot. Fortunately, I'd left the bedroom window cracked open, so I was able to climb up and remove the screen, and climb through the window in the house, hoping Mrs. Woods wasn't next door, looking out her kitchen window and see my naked butt.

I took a bath, put on clean clothes, and got a quick bite to eat. I was getting ready to leave when the whole ordeal suddenly hit me. I delivered a dead man to the hospital and received a baptism by way of his bodily fluids. The house was incredibly quiet, which amplified how weirdly disturbed I felt when I was directly confronted with the reality that none of us had any control over a single breath or heartbeat. Suddenly, my father popped into my mind, and I began to wonder if he had gone through a similar ordeal with his heart attack.

I left the house and started walking back to the hospital. As I approached the hospital corner, I could see my clothes still lying on the ground at the corner. I walked over to my pants, carefully picked them up, and removed my keys and wallet. I left the reeking clothes on the street corner as I walked to the emergency room and got a sack to carry my wet wallet in until I could dry it out. I made my way back to the station. Teddy was busy pumping gas for a customer, and everybody else was gone, so I got in my car and drove away. I arrived at my brother's place. His place was better known as The Fox Patrol, because of the girls who hung out there with my brother and his friend Les.

I knocked on the door, and Junior invited me in. He could tell something was bothering me. He asked, "What's up? I can tell something is going on." I laid out the whole story. He was amazed at what I told him but calmed me down.

My brother looked at me. "Normally, you are a pretty level-headed dude. I have something I want you to try."

"Okay," I replied.

He got up, went to the kitchen, and returned with a glass of punch. "Here, take this and wash it down. It's called a gray tab. It's a hit of acid, and it will definitely help put everything behind you."

I had no idea what acid was, so in my brother's usually organized, detailed manner, he explained. The gray tab was a mild, free-your-mind hallucinogenic. We dropped the acid as Junior put on the album *Are You Experienced?* by Jimi Hendrix. My mind and my world were about to change forever. I saw indescribable lights, waves, shapes and forms. My whole being was consumed and vibrating with the powerful music of Jimi Hendrix. After about four hours, I returned to the point where I was able to think and walk at the same time. It was early evening when my brother said, "Come on, let's go."

I had no idea what he was up to, but I got up and walked out the door with him. We headed down 5th Street toward the university, about three blocks away. It was dark, and everything was crazy cool with the reverberating sounds and strobing lights blending with kaleidoscope colors. I had never experienced anything like it. We reached the university and ended up at the small campus movie theater. By then, the effects of the acid had dwindled to a level where I was almost fully in control of my thoughts, but it felt like I was still traveling in another space. I was in a state where I felt like I could see all things, and I knew all things. Everything was crazy cool, then all the lights went out, the screen lit up, and the movie started.

The movie was a series of independent mini films on various subjects and events. The mini films showcased situations that moved from happy to sad, hilarious to tragic. It lasted about two hours, but I could have sat there all night watching the visual art unfold. We left the theater at about 10 p.m. and returned to Junior's place.

We talked a little longer, and then he put his big-brother arm around my shoulders, walked me to the door, and said goodbye. Before I left, he said to me, "Hey, man, I only let you turn on because I know you, and I know that you are not going to let any acid trip mess you up. So, don't go and do anything you can't undo."

I walked to my car, got in, and sat behind the wheel for a while, wishing I had some Jimi Hendrix to listen to since I had fallen in love with his huge, new, and powerful sound.

The Bewildering Idaho Desert

Not too long after my first acid trip, summer rolled around, and I started working back at the Site. This was a very good thing because I would be spending twelve hours of the day, 6 a.m. to 6 p.m., doing something constructive with great pay and not riding around drinking, smoking, or dropping acid. I had turned seventeen, meaning I still had to work in the central labor pool and could not work at the more interesting reactor facilities until I turned eighteen. Central was the Site entry point where the busloads of workers entered and left the entire facility. It was where all the administrative, medical, and general support facilities were located.

Some Friday paydays, I would skip the return bus ride to Pocatello and ride home with my good ol' buddy Hayward. Hayward was an older, middle-aged Black guy, and we shared a love for the blues. He drove a big, long, well-kept Deuce-N-A-Quarter, better known as a Buick Electra 225. We would zip down the long straight highway, sometimes hitting a hundred-plus miles an hour, and listen to the blues of Taj Mahal, Muddy Waters, or Howlin Wolf as Hayward scanned the highway for the reflective eyes of unsuspecting, doomed rabbits crossing the road.

One Friday, we were driving home, and Hayward turned off the highway onto a side road. I had no idea where we were headed. After driving for a short time, we pulled up in front of a building. It was an old bar with some cars and pickup trucks parked out front. We got out of the car, walked past a horse-hitching post, stepped upon an old, creaking wooden porch, and entered an old-time western bar with about fifteen people scattered about. It was a good-sized bar with a sawdust-covered floor, a horseshoe-shaped bar with several stools, and several tables and chairs spaced about. The bar looked like something out of a Hollywood western movie set. Hanging on the walls were stuffed heads of moose, elk, deer, and antelope, a large stuffed big-mouth bass, and a huge rainbow trout. There were also stuffed game birds like a pheasant, grouse, some duck, and a Canadian goose. There were also several oil paintings throughout the bar, paintings of nature scenes and animals, and a painting of the front of the bar with horses tied to the hitching post we walked past.

But there was one large, interesting painting hanging behind the bar. It was a large oil painting of a big tree. After closer inspection, I noticed something hanging from it. I leaned over the bar to get a closer look, and to my amazement, I could make out a Black man hanging from the tree. My heart was beating in my ears, and a cold chill raced through my body. Slowly, I looked toward the bartender, who was wearing a huge grin. "Go take a look out the back door," He said.

I turned away from the bar and walked to the back door. I looked out the window, and there it was: the same huge tree in the oil painting behind the bar. At that moment, I related to the story in Daniel 5, where God's finger writes on the wall in the presence of King Belshazzar: "Then all the color drained from the king's face, and he became alarmed. The joints of his hips gave way, and his knees began knocking together."

I was in a cowboy bar tucked away in the Idaho desert, and nobody knew I was there. It occurred to me that there was plenty of wilderness to bury a body, so it'd never be found. As I turned around, with my eyes nearly popping out of my head and my mouth wide open, everyone roared with laughter.

The bartender stopped laughing long enough to wipe tears from his eyes. "Don't worry, we're not planning any hangings today!"

More laughter erupted as I stood there, feeling like an idiot.

Afterward, the bartender told me the whole story. The Black man was hung because he was a horse thief and got caught. It could have been a White man hanging there because horse theft was not tolerated, no matter who the thief.

I recovered from the shock, and Hayward and I stayed until about 3 a.m. Hayward played some blues with the electric guitar and speaker he had in the car, and everyone in the bar genuinely enjoyed it. We also listened to country and western music, played darts, and shot a lot of pool. We drank whiskey with beer chasers, mixed drinks, and even some cowboy moonshine. I also ate some of the best BBQ ever from the pit in the back of the bar. I still remember that evening as one of my most memorable evenings ever—two Black guys partying with a bunch of cowboys and cowgirls and some crazy desert rats.

Dark Deed Comes to Light

The summer job at the Site ended, school was getting ready to start, and things got very interesting with a girl named Jenny. Jenny was a cute Black girl who lived next door with Mr. and Mrs. Woods, her uncle and aunt. My mother repeatedly warned me about leaving her alone, but I didn't listen. One day, Jenny told me she was pregnant. The terrible news rattled me and shook me to the very core of my soul. I became consumed with Jenny's horrible news as I churned it over and over in my mind. She told me she hadn't had a period for over two months. I couldn't sleep. I couldn't eat. But I had no problem drinking and trying to drown the miserable news at every opportunity. I wish I had listened to my mother. Her words echoed in my head: "You better leave that girl alone!"

I had been exposed to the sexual realm in my very early days at the speakeasies with my dad. Sometimes, I would see scantily clad women exiting their working rooms, and to attract more business, they would expose themselves by only wearing panties and a bra. But my greatest sexual exposure was during a summer vacation in Portland, Oregon.

We visited one of my mother's relatives, and there was a beautiful young daughter everyone called Bee. She looked like a cross between a young Vanessa Williams and Halle Berry. She was a year older and a head taller than me. She had light, honey-brown hair, perfect symmetrical facial features, and hazel eyes, and she wore sun dresses that looked like they had to be spray painted on her perfectly formed athletic body. But oddly enough, the girl was a rugged tomboy.

One day, we returned to the house from running around Portland, but no one was home. She grabbed me by the hand and led me to a room on the third floor, where she instructed, encouraged, and guided me through some erotic scenarios. When we were finished, I was no longer the innocent Pocatello boy that started the visit. When I returned home, the puppy love romance that used to exist between Jenny and me transformed into a whole different lustful reality. Jenny was just along for the ride as I replayed variations of the erotic scenarios I learned in Portland.

Time passed, and Christmas was right around the corner when I received the biggest Christmas present of my life. One afternoon, I met Jenny in the alley, and she told me she wasn't pregnant. She told me she had a miscarriage, and she said nothing more. She looked a little strange, and I tried to question her, but she quickly turned away and started walking toward the house. The scare with Jenny truly threw me for a loop. My soul was so disturbed that I was close to dropping out of school and wanting to run away.

Then came the seemingly good news that Jenny *wasn't* pregnant because she had a miscarriage. Was it really good news? The thought of her body expelling a dead baby put me on a whole different level of low. I thought about something my mom often said: "God works in mysterious ways." I couldn't believe that God would take a baby's life to accommodate *me*. I became so confused. I couldn't maintain a focus on anything. I stopped playing football, and booze became my only confidant, friend, and escape.

During my senior year at Poky High, I turned eighteen. My work status was upgraded at the Site so I could legally work at the nuclear reactor sites and make more money. I had plenty of funds to help my mom pay for school expenses and plenty left to party with. I was starting my senior year. The Jenny trauma was over, there's some peace from my dad's death, and I wanted to go to school and play football with a great bunch of guys. Fortunately, I listened to my brother, Darwin, Jimmy, and several older Black guys in Pocatello. Whether I partied with them or not, they were always on me about staying in school. Plus, my mom constantly reminded me, "You better stay in school because if you don't know much, you can't do much, and if you can't do much, don't ask for much."

I had planned to join the Air Force after high school. I was highly influenced by some of the Air Force dudes who traveled to Pocatello from Mountain Home Air Force Base near Boise, the state capital, so I was very excited about getting through my last year of high school.

A couple of weeks before school started, I left my mom's house, and as I headed to my car, Jenny came out of her uncle's house. We paused and looked at each other. We hadn't talked to each other in the past couple of months, so I headed her way. "Hey there. You look nice. Where are you headed? You want a ride?" She accepted my offer, and we got into my car.

We rode around a bit, then to the Red Steer Drive-in for a great hamburger. We ended up on the top level of Ross Park. Soon, we were in the backseat of my 1958 Oldsmobile Super 88. A vision of my mother flashed in my mind, and I could hear her paraphrasing one of her bible verses, like Luke 8:17: "You better be careful because what is done in the dark will come out in the light."

After a while, I dropped Jenny off at her original destination. It was Saturday, and I was supposed to be at the school for the follow-up after a Friday game, but I didn't go. Suddenly, I became very disturbed, so I decided to go over to Jimmy's and tell him about the escapade in the back seat of my car. When I told him, he put his big hand on my shoulder, swaying me back and forth. "Way to go, Papa!" Then he erupted into his monster laughter.

I was upset after Jimmy's reality check, so I jumped into partying. I started drinking and smoking everything that came my way. I don't know how I made it home, but it was Sunday afternoon, and I was awakened by my mother returning from church.

I was passed out across the bed, and I could hear my mom yelling at me and shaking me. Then she grabbed me like a rag doll, forced me off the bed, and stripped off all my clothes. Once she rendered me buck naked, she steered me into the bathroom and forced me into a bathtub of steaming hot water. My entire body was consumed in burning pain when the hot water hit the mysterious welts and bruises all over my body. I didn't remember getting into any fights or falling out of my car, so I had no idea why I was so bruised and beaten up. This had happened before, and when I finally sobered up, I remained very disturbed about the mystery. Years later, on a Pocatello visit, my mother told me she would use a razor-sharpening belt and beat me after I came home throwing up around the house, peeing in my chest of drawers and clothes hamper, and then passing out. My mother became fed up with my terrible behavior. Behavior that had become the norm for me.

Key block for Presley Vann.

It was October, and school was in full swing. Football season was coming to an end. I was do well in all my classes, and I still had some money left from summer work at the Site. Things were going well. At the end of one school day, I was talking with a girl at her locker. Jenny rushed up in a rage, pushed the girl away, and slammed her locker door shut. She started yelling and cursing at me with furious anger as she shouted out, "I'll be damned if you are going to mess around with this White b***h while I'm carrying your damn baby!" I froze in a state of shock. Everything seemed surreal, as if I were floating in a bad dream. A vision of my mother appeared, and I heard her say, "I warned you. What you do in the dark will come out in the light." Then, a vision of Jimmy appeared, laughing and calling me Papa.

When I returned to my senses, I looked around, and a crowd of students had gathered. The girl I was talking to was leaning against the wall of lockers, clutching her shirt in total shock. She, too, was staring at me like I had the black plague. The crowd parted like the Red Sea as Jenny stomped away, yelling, cursing, and crying. All I could think was, Oh my God, my mother was right again! I didn't know what to do. I stood frozen near the girl's locker. She approached me, put her hand on my shoulder, and asked if I was okay. I nodded. Then, she walked away. In a daze, I started walking down the hall in the opposite direction of Jenny's exit.

One of my druggy buddies ran up to me and said, "Wow, man! That was intense! I thought she was going to mess you up! Are you okay? You wanna go get a buzz?"

I nodded, and we took off.

When we made it to his car, I changed my mind. All I could think about was how disappointed my mother was going to be with me. It hadn't been that long since school started that Jenny and I had been passionately clinging together in the back seat of my Super 88. It wasn't that long after my first scare with Jenny that a casual conversation went terribly in the wrong direction. We finally started talking again after her miscarriage, and all I wanted to do was apologize to her honestly. And now the bill had come due for that lustful moment.

My mind was in a whirlwind. I couldn't eat or sleep, and all I wanted to do was stay buzzed to try to block it out, but strangely enough, school was a weird, welcome distraction. Even though I got several strange looks in the hallways, nobody dared to say anything to me, or they stood a good chance of getting a fist in their face.

I saw Jenny in the hallway a short time after her attack. I approached her to talk, but she completely ignored me. I wanted to sort things out, but she was having none of it. I knew that one day, this whole thing was going to blow up with her belly—literally—and my mother and her uncle were going to have a total fit.

I couldn't take it any longer. One day, I went home from school, walked up to my mom, and blurted out, "Jenny's pregnant!"

Mom replied, "Well, what are you going to do?"

"I don't know."

She walked away, shaking her head.

I felt relieved and terrible, all at the same time.

Time passed, and it was right before Christmas. Jenny was about three months pregnant. She was barely showing, but that didn't matter when my mother and I went next door to buttheads with Buddy Woods, her uncle. Mr. Woods answered the door, and he gave me the stare-down. It was obvious he knew, and I felt like he wanted to shoot me and bury me in my mom's backyard. Our so-called talk didn't go well from the beginning. Mrs. Woods did nothing but cry. Mr. Woods kept asking when we were getting married, and my mother didn't say a word. So, to shake things up, I blurted out, "Well, since we don't have our own place, I guess we'll move in with you and stay in the basement."

My statement brought Mr. Woods to his senses, and he realized that his great marriage plans would not work. My mom and several others convinced Mr. Woods that it would probably be best if I were to complete school and Jenny should go to the home for unwed mothers near Boise and have the baby and then come home.

I thought about something my mom said: "I told you and told you that all wrong will be repaid. It's not because God is angry at you, but because the bible says that all sin carries its own consequences, and now there's a debt you have to pay." After thinking about it, the title of Clarence Carter's song kept flashing in my mind, "If I Could Turn Back the Hands of Time." It kept flashing over and over in my mind, leaving me looking down a long road of uncertainty.

Time passed, and I graduated from Poky High. While driving one day in town, I wondered if I would continue seeing all the wonderful guys I played football with. I figured I would continue seeing all my enlightenment buddies—Teddy, Larry, Thane, and Daniel were always around.

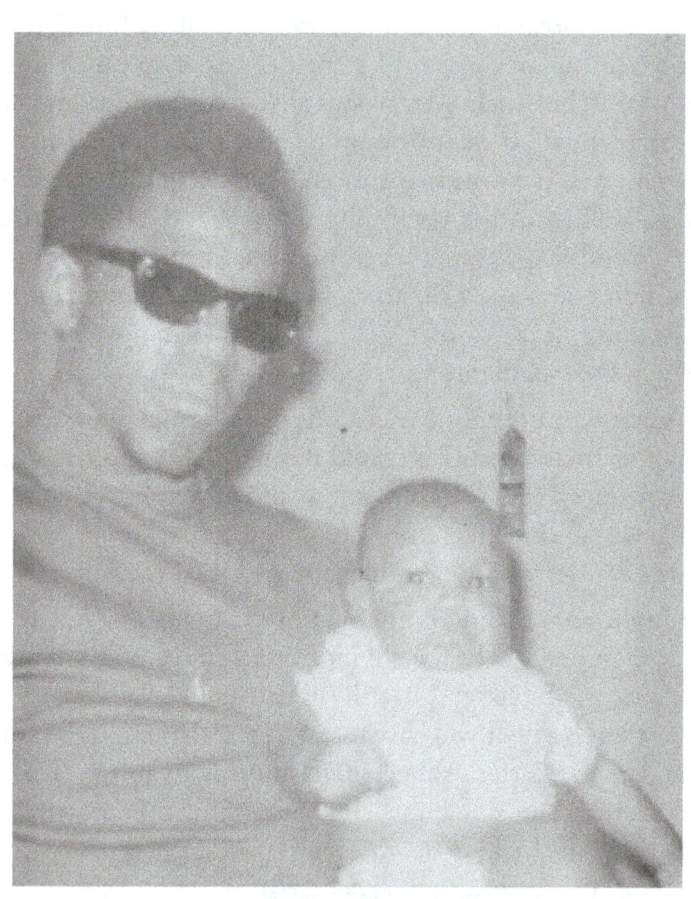

Me and baby Anthony

CHAPTER
8

STARTING COLLEGE WITH A FLOP

On My Way to College

Mr. Woods and I returned to Pocatello from the home for unwed mothers with Jenny and baby Anthony. We parked, and I helped Jenny and Anthony get out of the car and into the Woods' house. I made the necessary trips carrying Jenny and the baby's stuff into the house. My mom heard us drive up, so she joined Mr. and Mrs. Woods with Jenny and Anthony. I left like I was going to get more stuff, but instead, I got into my car and took off looking for Darwin, Jimmy, Daniel, or somebody so I could get my drink on with. I was fed up with Mr. Woods and his pressuring marriage talk. With Jenny and baby Anthony back in Pocatello, I had to decide between entering the Air Force or attending Idaho State University.

I finally ran into Darwin; strangely enough, he was looking for me. I parked in front of the Jim Dandy Club and got into Darwin's car. He told me he needed my help. He had a job to do for Clide, delivering a package in the Chubbuck area. I found this a little strange because Chubbuck was an area where Black folks usually didn't go. Black folks would go to the Chubbuck area to go to the Green Triangle, a restaurant that served some good food, especially thick, juicy steaks. There didn't seem to be much of a problem getting food from the restaurant. But there seemed to be an issue when Black folks would go there to party on the weekends, resulting in fights, knifings, or shootings.

We got out of Darwin's car and walked into the Club. Darwin left me to meet Clide, so I stayed in the café and ordered a chicken drumstick basket with fries and a beer. I was listening to "Sittin' on The Dock of the Bay" by Otis Redding and enjoying my food when Darwin returned from the bar area. He walked to the door and motioned for me to follow him. I got up with my food basket, still eating the tasty chicken, and walked out the door. We got in Darwin's car and took off. He said to me, "I have to make a run and drop off a package, and I need a lookout. You think you can do it?" I replied, "*Sure, whatever you need.*"

He said, "I am driving out to Cowboy Town and dropping off a package. There's a gun under the seat if needed."

I replied, "Okay, let's go!"

In about twenty minutes, we drove to a nice house sitting off the road by way of a circular driveway. We parked, Darwin got out, walked to the front door, knocked, and a man answered. I could faintly see Darwin handing off the package, and he returned to the car with a small paper sack. Darwin handed the sack to me and told me to open it as we drove away.

I opened the sack and pulled out a pint bottle of clear liquid.

"Well, open it! Take a drink and pass it here," Darwin said.

I twisted off the cap and took a drink. At first, I felt nothing, then I suddenly felt like I had drunk liquid fire. I started gagging, choking, and coughing, and everything started spinning as if I was going to black out. Darwin started laughing as he snatched the bottle from my hand before I dropped it, and he took a drink. Darwin drove a four-speed, and it started to sputter after the strong moonshine shook him, but he recovered and continued driving. We made our way back to Lander Street, had another drink, put the liquid fire under the seat, and went to Tiny's.

I eventually made it home. My mother told me Mr. Woods was extremely upset that I had taken off. I simply didn't care because that old man was not going to tell me what to do, and he was not going to force me into marriage. My mom also told me that there was a letter from the ISU registration office. I was late filling out an ISU admission application, but I was still expecting to hear back from them.

Registration for school started in April, and it was May. So, it definitely looked like I was going to college since a couple of my

Black buddies had talked me out of going into the Air Force. I'm still not sure that staying home would be a smart decision. I picked up some information from Mrs. Purce regarding a business scholarship with affirmative action money and a work-study program. It looked like the program would take care of what to do for a college major and supply some desired funds.

My mom filled out and submitted paperwork to the Union Pacific Railroad and Social Security so I could continue receiving funds for as long as I was in college. I was also not too concerned about the draft and Vietnam, with a draft number of 358 out of 365. My mom seemed much more pleased about me staying home and going to school and not going into military service, especially during wartime. She told me some disturbing stories about some of the nurses she worked with and their association with family and friends who had lost young men to the war.

I barely made the registration deadline for classes, but I was fortunate enough to get everything done. All I had to do was make a true commitment to go to school. After I had completed the admission process, it was time to go and party. I made my way over to Jimmy's to spread the good news. When I got there, Darwin and several other people were there. I told everybody I was officially registered at ISU, and everyone congratulated me. I stayed and had a couple of mixed drinks, and then I wanted to tell my brother the good news.

I made it to Junior's house and told him the good news. He and his friends were genuinely happy for me. They were going to a bar called Juck's and invited me to come.

I had driven by the bar many times, and every time, I wrote it off as a country and western bar, so I never stopped. When we walked in the door, "In-A-Gadda-Da-Vida" by Iron Butterfly was playing on the jukebox, and I instantly fell in love with the place, its wooden floor, and the old-style bar. It was a good-sized place with booths lining the walls and tables and chairs spaced about the floor. This place was amazing, loaded with college students, hippies, and druggies.

We picked a booth to sit in, and Junior and one of the girls went to the bar to buy pitchers of beer. I walked over to the jukebox to check out the music. There were great songs like "All Along the Watchtower" by The Jimi Hendrix Experience, "White Room" by Cream, "Time Has Come Today" by The Chambers Brothers, and "MacArthur Park" by Richard Harris. This great bar had been under my nose all this time, and I didn't know it! Unfortunately, it would become a frequent watering hole for me. It was about 9 p.m. when we got there, and after what seemed like no time at all, the bartender was flashing the lights, signaling the 2 a.m. closing time.

We wobbled to our cars as we all said goodnight to each other, and I climbed into my car and drove away. I drove by Jimmy's and saw several silhouettes moving about the shaded windows. I pulled over and was getting ready to get out, but something stirred inside me. I thought about my mom, Jenny, and Anthony. Suddenly, the party light grew very dim within me. I had no desire to continue to party, and I yearned to see Jenny and Anthony. But it was after 3 a.m. I'd also had too much to drink, and I didn't want to lay eyes on Mr. Woods, so it was home for me.

College Became a Party

College was in full swing, and so was I with my daily classes. I enrolled in twelve units of general Ed classes, enough to maintain my student status and keep me off the draft board's radar. I was in the swing of college, getting up every day and making it to all my classes. Everything was going well until I was approached to join the Kappa Alpha Psi fraternity.

Now, I want to make it clear from the beginning that the frat was not the problem, but some of the established members were a problem for me. The frat was primarily Black dudes, most of them going to school on athletic scholarships and a few on academic scholarships. Ninety-five percent of them were from out of state, and the other 5 percent were locals.

It was mid-September when I attended my first Kappa party. Sometime later, I moved out of my mother's house and into a room in the Kappa House, which turned out to be a huge mistake. I was mysteriously moved up the Kappa House room availability list.

At the end of October, I was no longer studying. The only class I was attending was my college algebra class, which I enjoyed and was doing well in. I had not seen my mother, Jenny, or Anthony in a while. Practically every night was a party night and extended into the next morning. I had set up several drug contacts and was making money on the side. I don't remember how much money I had invested. People came by and dropped off money. Things were rolling by, and I felt like a prisoner in the Kappa room. I didn't want to leave my room, and when I did leave, it was only to attend my algebra class or to hook up with Daniel to get high. I had gotten myself into a real mess.

One day, I broke away and went to my mother's house. I turned the doorknob, but the door was locked, which was very unusual. I knocked, and my mom answered. I entered the house, closed the door, and said, "Well, I am glad you are home since I don't have my key and the door was locked."

She replied, "Well, you have been gone so long, I didn't know if you were going to come up in here all messed up." She then paraphrased one of her bible verses: "You know, a foolish son grieves his mother."

I am sure she was talking about Proverbs 10:1, "A wise son makes a glad father, but a foolish son is the grief of his mother."

My heart dropped as I stood there looking at my poor mother and feeling like a fool. I was so tired and asked, "Mom, may I stay home, please?"

She replied, "Yes, you can stay here, as long as you don't come up in here acting like a fool, 'cause I'm not going to have it!" I said, "Don't worry, Mom, I didn't bring the fool with me."

She told me I had some mail from the school. I walked over to a wooden where the new mail was placed, a bowl I'd made in wood shop back in junior high school. I picked up a letter from ISU with the words "Academic Probation Notice" on it. A cold chill immediately rushed through my body. It was from the Dean's Office stating that I needed to make an appointment, and failure to do so would prompt the office to report my immediate availability to the draft board. Reading the letter threw my heart into shock. I rushed to the phone, called, and scheduled an appointment for the next morning. My timing to return home appeared mysteriously perfect, and it left me feeling a little strange.

My mom asked, "When did you last see the baby?" I turned and gave her my typical blank, dumb look and said nothing. She said, "Well, you need to get over there and see that baby and let Jenny and Buddy know you're still alive. Buddy's been doing nothing but asking about you, and I said you're in school." I stood there and continued giving her my dumb look, and finally said, "Okay, but would it be all right if I take a bath first?" She said to go ahead.

I finished my bath, dressed, and reluctantly went to Mr. Woods's house next door to see Jenny and Anthony. When I knocked on the door. Mrs. Woods answered and welcomed me in. She informed me that Mr. Woods was not home. She had no idea how relieved that made me.

As we walked downstairs, I lied and told Mrs. Woods I had not been around because of school but had moved back home.

I stayed with Jenny and Anthony for a couple of hours and was truly blessed that Mr. Woods didn't return while I was visiting. When Anthony fell asleep, I returned to my mom's house. I sat on the back porch in peaceful darkness, thinking about my mom, Mr. Woods, Jenny, the baby, the dean's office, and the night my daddy died.

Suddenly, my mind flooded with images of bleeding and dying soldiers in the Vietnam jungles. I began having strange thoughts about the math I'd learned and come to love. And then my mind bounced to my abandoned Kappa House room and all the stuff I left behind. Suddenly, the title of the song "Worst That Could Happen" by Brooklyn Bridge popped into my mind. Even though the song is about a guy whining about a girl, I related the title to the worst thing that could happen to me would be my mother not being around to help pick up the pieces from another mess I've made.

It's amazing how much I depend upon my mother, and I didn't even realize it. But what I had come to realize is my mother's persistent strength. And her persistent strength is a direct product of her resilient, unwavering faith. That faith is soundly based on the only true living God, His word, and Jesus, which she has always talked about.

9

REBOUNDING IN COLLEGE

College—Getting Back on Track

The next morning, I made my way to the Dean's Office. I was a little nervous but more embarrassed than anything. The dean caught me off guard when he came straight at me and asked, "So, Presley, tell me what's going on?" I was amazed by how personable and genuinely concerned he seemed.

"Sir, I have no excuse. I got off on the wrong foot with the wrong people. I was born and raised in Pocatello and have been around ISU all my life. One of my best friend's fathers was the head football coach and athletic director here. Since my elementary school days, I had spent a huge amount of time at ISU with him, but I had no idea about ISU until I started attending it. It is totally different from high school, and I allowed myself to lose focus, and I got swept away."

The dean responded, "Well, you have a choice to leave school, and your student availability status will be reported to the draft board, or you can agree to join a probationary recovery program. The program consists of repeating some classes, taking a mandatory core class, progress monitoring, and reporting." I said I'd gladly join the program.

The dean asked me why I kept up with the math class despite allowing my other classes to fall by the wayside. I explained that I had always liked math despite struggling with. I was glad to have an excellent instructor who helped me understand it better, so I liked it.

Even though my academic strength was in the liberal arts, I wanted to prove that I could do math. I told him that I accepted math as a challenge and that my goal was to take calculus. He told me that he hoped I was serious about getting back on track and told me to see the secretary, sign an agreement, and receive instructions on the recovery program process. We got up and shook hands. He walked me to his office door and said, "Presley, remember, it's a very short pen stroke from 1-S to 1-A." I could not believe that the meeting went so well. I told myself that things would improve, and I would do exactly what I was supposed to do.

I left the dean's office and went to the administration building to hand in the paperwork. I waited for a while, then a lady came out and met me, and we went into a conference room where we reviewed my record. I was surprised when she said I had a class withdrawal for my English and philosophy classes, but I was not surprised with the F in my PE swimming class, and I had a B in algebra. I had no idea where the withdrawals came from. I left the lady with a revised schedule for the 1969 spring semester. I would repeat English, philosophy, and PE and move on to trigonometry for math and a new study core class. When I completed everything, I summoned the courage from somewhere and went to the Kappa House to get my belongings.

When I'd left the Kappa House, I'd walked away and abandoned everything in my room. I took only my math books and the clothes on my back. I couldn't have cared less about anything else, including the rest of my schoolbooks. I had been gone from the Kappa House for a while, but fortunately, the Kappa brothers boxed up my stuff and stored it in the basement. Nothing was missing or destroyed, and fortunately, no one had sold my textbooks. I put everything in my car and I took off to my mom's house.

Time passed, and it was a couple of weeks before the end of the 1968 fall semester and heading into Christmas. I was so excited that I would have started school that day if I could. The new semester would start in the second week of January, which gave me about a month to keep it all together and not do anything stupid.

Second Semester Starts on the Right Track

I made it through the break before the start of the new school year. It was January 1969, a new year, and I felt like I had been given a new lease on life. I only drank an occasional beer and consumed no other mind-altering substances.

I was at home, hanging out with my mom, and frequently visited Jenny and Anthony next door. I had been able to fend off Mr. Woods's marriage plans with my plans to continue with school. While I was going to school and staying with my mom, Jenny and Anthony would continue to stay with the Woods.

I was excited that the second semester was finally starting. I faithfully made it to all my classes. In between classes, I spent study time at the student union building. I was focused and not messing around. All my other classes were successfully moving along except for trigonometry. I understood the basic trigonometric functions and concepts. But then I ran into this thing called the unit circle and translating between degrees to radians—what the hell was Pi all about? I went to the math aid center for help, but I was still falling behind in finishing homework. The next test was coming quickly, and I was not ready.

My lifelong Black friend Evans was an engineering major at ISU, so I hit him up for help. We would meet everywhere, including my mom's house, his mom's house, and the student union building. He was even doing my homework so I wouldn't fall behind as I struggled. Sometimes, I would leave Evans, drive away, pull over, and start crying. I wanted this so bad, but I was missing something. I did everything Evans said, but understanding the unit circle concepts kept escaping me. I desperately wanted to succeed, so one day, I was thinking about my mom, and then I did something I wouldn't normally do. I prayed. It was more than prayer; I would beg and plead for God to help me to understand this unit circle and radian thing and successfully move on with my trigonometry.

One day, I was meeting with Evans and going to give up, but Evans urged me not to quit. I silently started praying as we continued with the tutoring, and a light turned on about something he said during the study—the unit conversion differences between degrees and radians and how Pi figured in with arch measurements started to make sense. As we continued studying and reviewing my homework,

I began to understand and started doing the exercises and homework on my own. Soon, I was doing many different exercises and practicing as many problems as I could. I also continued going to the tutoring center to get practice problems and ask questions. I became so excited and confident about my math that it was all I wanted to do.

I was still in general Ed classes, but I now wanted to change my prospective major from business to math, and I owed it all to Evans. If it had not been for Evans sacrificing his time for me, I would have dropped trigonometry, and that would have been the end of my interest in math, science, and engineering. Because of Evans, I would eventually pursue electronics in the Marine Corps schools, and I would eventually have an extremely successful electronics engineering career as a civilian.

Getting Through My Second Semester

Even though I had to repeat some classes due to the withdrawals and the F, the second semester started on the right foot, and everything went extremely well. I maintained around a 2.75 GPA and knew I could continue with good grades if I kept my head on straight. Soon, I was in finals week and at the end of the semester.

I set up my class schedule for the summer, my third semester. Even though I had to use the current semester for a class cleanup, it was okay because I felt confident that I was on the right track. At the time, I wanted to do something in electronics like my dad, but, at the time, there was no Bachelor's electrical engineering degree (BSEE) at Idaho State University, and a BSEE program wouldn't happen until sometime after 1996. However, with my new fondness for math, I was entertaining other possibilities in the Department of Engineering at ISU.

Besides school, I maintained a great relationship with my mother. She enjoyed that I was sane and sober and not coming home wasted at all hours of the night. I frequently came home to find her reading her bible. We would talk, and she'd eventually say, "Well, you're not going to church anymore, but are you reading your bible?"

Once again, I sat there, dumbfounded and silent. "You know," she'd say, "the devil is roaming and looking for some fool to take hold of. You better be careful." I am sure she was referring to 1 Peter 5:8, "Be sober, be vigilant; because your adversary the devil walks about like a roaring lion, seeking whom he may devour."

Even though I was doing much better, my mom was still a little leery of me. I know she absolutely and unconditionally loved me, so I was hoping she would start to relax a little more when we were together, especially since I was earnestly trying to continue to do the right thing. I also wanted to tell her about how I desperately prayed to God for help when I was stuck with my trigonometry, but I held back.

I swear He answered my prayers because the impossible happened. Even though I was confused about who God truly is, there's one thing I knew for sure, and that was, if I had not thought about my mom at the time, I wouldn't have called on God for help. I did like she'd always said about opening my heart and sincerely calling on God for help in times of need, and it looked like she was right again.

CHAPTER
10

JOURNEY TO DEFLATION

Starting My Third Semester

The 1969 spring semester came and went. I wanted to take a math class in the summer of 1969, but the lure of making a lot of money over the summer at the Site was too much to ignore. Since I decided not to go to summer school, I went to the tutoring center, picked up as many pre-calculus lessons and problems as possible, and borrowed a pre-calculus class textbook. I figured I could at least get a head start on pre-calculus during the summer to prepare for the fall semester.

Before long, summer was over, and the 1969 fall semester started. I picked up a nice grant from school and made plenty of money from the Site. I spent a good amount of time with my mother, Jenny, and Anthony. I hardly spent any time with Jimmy and Darwin, but a little time with Daniel at Juck's. I was driven to get to school and passed all my classes.

Since I worked at the nuclear engineering testing site in the desert, I visited the school's nuclear engineering department to find a possible job. I talked to some students and a professor and asked about job openings or work-study programs. They said no, but I might want to check at the computer center. I immediately headed to the center. When I arrived, several people were working around computers.

A lady behind the counter asked if she could help me, and I told her I was there to check out a possible job. A gentleman overheard our conversation, came out of his office, and walked over to the counter. The gentleman asked if I had any computer operations experience. I told him no, but I had work experience at the nuclear testing site in the Arco Desert as a data coordinator for engineers and scientists. The gentleman seemed pleased to hear that and told me that if I could get a character reference, I might be able to train for an evening position in computer operation support.

I left the computer center beaming with hope. I didn't know what to do about the character reference, so I jumped into my car and drove straight to my brother's place. When I arrived at his house, I told him the great news and asked if he could help me get a character reference. He told me he would check into it and get back to me the next day.

Junior asked if I would like to stay and have dinner with him and his guest, and I accepted. Junior was a good cook because he definitely paid attention to our mom. He had prepared a tasty roasted chicken, seasoned mashed potatoes, green beans, and dinner rolls. The dinner was great, and we finished it with a bottle of spendy red wine. I stayed for a while and listened to him and his friends as they continued practicing a classical piece, his flute accompanied by a violin and cello. My brother played a variety of musical styles, but his heart was focused on classical composers like Beethoven, Bach, Lindell, and Haydn.

Listening to the trio reminded me of a time when our mother worked for the Markhams, a wealthy White family that lived in Pocatello. Mr. Markham owned an advertising company that covered a good portion of the western states. Our mother cleaned house for Mrs. Markham, and she would also serve during dinner parties and special events at their nice house. One evening, I helped my mom at a dinner party with Senator Frank Church, John R. Simplot, and a few other dignitaries in attendance. Along with the excellent food and expensive wine and cognac, my brother played his flute, a girl played a viola, and another girl played a cello. I don't recall the classical piece they played, but their harmonious sound captured everyone's attention. I felt extremely privileged and proud while sneaking shooters of expensive wine and cognac.

The next day, I was sitting in the student union building. My brother approached me and told me to go to the computer center and that I should have the job. I found out that he had talked to a math professor who played guitar in one of his jamming groups, and he gave the computer center a character reference for me. I rushed over to the center and met with the supervisor. We set up my training and work schedule, and I asked if I could hang out and observe until my next class.

I was doing great, enrolled in pre-calculus with my other required classes, maintaining a 2.65 GPA, working at a dream job, and nothing could be better. Looking back, I wonder how it all happened. How was I now walking on the straight and narrow where, previously, I was tripping all over myself? I learned from my mother that she and my sister Mildred, in Kansas City, Missouri, prayed over me by long-distance phone calls, and I believe their prayers were being answered.

Working Through My Third and Fourth Semesters

The 1969 fall semester ended in fine fashion. I registered for the 1970 Spring semester and was extremely excited about taking Calculus I. I also selected a tutor for the semester and gave Evans a long-deserved break.

Christmas was the following week, and I loved the Christmas season—the snow and the wonderful seasonal aromas. I could stop by anybody's house in The Triangle and be invited in to share some fantastic Christmas music, food, and drinks. I loved all the great songs on the radio, like my all-time favorite Christmas song, "Little Drummer Boy" by Harry Simeone Chorale, "The Christmas Song" by Nat King Cole, "White Christmas" by Bing Crosby, and "Have Yourself a Merry Little Christmas" by Frank Sinatra. My mom also had a great collection of Christmas blues songs like "Lonesome Christmas" by Lowell Fulson, "Please Come Home for Christmas" by Charles Brown, and "Christmas Comes but Once A Year" by Amos Milburn.

I ran around town a bit but returned to my mom's house. She was at home and very excited about my success in school and my retaining my job at the college computer center. I was planning on having a simple conversation with her, but instead, out of the blue, she asked, "When was the last time you went to church?"

Once again, I stood with a familiar dumbfounded, goofy look. "I don't know, it's been a while." She replied, "You know, this is not the way you were raised. If it weren't for the Lord's blessing on you, you wouldn't have that job or nothing else." How could I doubt her after all that's happened lately, but I was still skeptical, I just didn't know?.

I made it through Christmas of 1969 and the New Year of 1970 without messing up. Before long, the 1970 Spring semester had started and ended. I didn't know what to expect with Calculus I, but it ended up not being as tough as I thought. I stayed close to my tutor and finished the semester with a B. The remainder of my classes were more of a nuisance since I immersed myself in math and the computer center and I didn't waste any time with Jimmy, Darwin, or Daniel, and I didn't go to Juck's.

I registered for the 1970 fall semester. Finals were over, and the semester was about to end. It had been well over a semester since I'd dropped the Kappa Alpha Psi pledging, being one less thing to be concerned with during the semester. The fraternity's history was admirable, but I encountered too many hypocritical so-called brothers for me to continue pledging.

Several Black dudes were running around campus spouting their "Black Power" stuff and making all kinds of noise about race issues. But when the sun went down, several of them got high and jammed with White girls. I'm not talking about all the Black members, but several Black dudes wore two faces. Again, several Black guys were serious about getting an education, so I'm not throwing the entire frat under the bus.

My state of mind was not to worry about the frat, race issues, or any other distractions but to keep my head on straight, stay focused, and keep my eye on the prize of getting good grades and making sure I passed all my classes and watch my academic probation fade away in my rearview mirror.

Making it Through My Fifth Semester

School had been in full swing for a couple of months for the 1970 fall semester, my fifth semester. Again, I wish I could have taken all math courses, but I couldn't. I was taking Probability and Calculus II. I was experiencing difficulties with the more advanced concepts of sequences, series, and parametric equations, but I was confident I'd figure it out with my tutor.

My tutor was a math major named Sidney, a really cute, dynamic girl. She looked a little bit like Jacqueline Kennedy in her 5'11", shapely, athletic frame. She sported shoulder-length, honey-blond hair that glistened in the sunlight. She was also a tutor for some of the Black athletes, so she became a huge source of contention between me and a couple of the knuckleheads who were brothers in the Kappa Alpha Phi fraternity.

A couple of the Black athletes had their noses wide open for Sidney and were always sniffing around. They constantly tried to draw her away, but she would shut them down. Being Pocatello home-grown, I had a huge advantage over all the Black dudes who constantly pressured her. After a tutoring session, I would invite her to my mom's house and treat her to some delicious leftovers and dessert. Then we would relax, watch TV, listen to music, and talk.

As we progressed through the semester, a couple of jealous Black athletes interrupted our tutoring sessions more and more. When we were together, they would barge in, start talking to her, and completely ignore me. If I said anything, they would glare at me like I had the plague, not saying a word to me, but kept talking to Sidney until she shut them down. The encounters were getting worse and worse to where one particular Black basketball player would confront us, and he would immediately start calling me several bad names that spewed out of his cesspool mouth.

One evening, Sidney and I were in the student union building for a tutoring session. It was about 7 p.m., and a few students were sitting in the surrounding sections. I looked up, and this one particularly obnoxious Black basketball player had approached us. This guy and I already shared a bad history from my Kappa pledging days, so he kept me in his sights. On one Kappa occasion, all the fraternity brothers were supposed to hide from the pledgers because we were granted "Big Brother for A Day." If we caught a fraternity brother, they were to do as we ordered, but within reason. All the pledged brothers agreed to go along for the granted window of time, except for this tall, lanky, ignorant fool who was now walking toward us. One evening, I tore into this dude at a Kappa meeting, and we almost got into it. I let him know how much of a hypocrite he was and that he was a brother to morons that put up with his hypocrisy. Well, needless to say, that was the end of my Kappa pledge days.

I could tell there was going to be an unavoidable confrontation with this idiot. He walked up to me and started yelling, "Hey, what's up, little n***a!"

My heart dropped. "Hey, man, why don't you continue on about your business and leave me alone."

He replied, "n***a, the only thing I am going to leave you is a knot upside your head!"

I could see Sidney out of the corner of my eye, and she was terrified. I immediately scooted out of my seat in front of him.

"Okay, fool! Hold on, I got something for you!" He placed his books on the table and turned toward me with his arms at his side, and his fists balled up.

I said, "Okay, hold on, here you go!" I stuck out my left arm and gestured for him to stop, which he did.

He stood still, looking at me strangely as I took a few steps back and quickly unbuttoned the top button on my pants. I stuck my right hand down the back of my pants as though I were poking my middle finger up my poop chute. Then I pulled my hand out and pointed my middle finger at the tall idiot, who looked completely bewildered.

"Okay, fool! Here I come! I'm going to write my name on your big, black forehead!"

As I walked briskly toward him, he yelled, "What's wrong with you, fool? Stay away from me!" He looked terrified as he started backing up faster and faster.

I kept pace by walking faster and faster toward him. Eventually, he turned and ran full stride toward the big glass doors in front of the student union building. He hit the front doors, pushed them wide open, and ran out and down the stairs with me right behind him.

He ran across the rolling grass mounds in front of the student union building, and I kept pace. As he was running, he turned and shouted, "You're crazy, man! Get away from me! Leave me alone!"

I shouted back, "I'm going to write my name, fool!"

When he reached the sidewalk, he kept running for a short distance and then cut between parked cars and cut across 5th Street. Cars hit their brakes as he entered the street with me on his tail.

We both made it across the street, where I chased him in and out of Elmor's restaurant. He kept running down the sidewalk before running back across 5th Street, stopping traffic again, and then chased him in and out of a coffee shop. Finally, he stopped.

It appeared that he was about to take a stand. I ran straight at him, waving my finger in the air and screaming like a madman. That was enough to send him off running again.

He made it to the corner of Benton and 5th, where he ran diagonally across the busy intersection, once again, bringing traffic to a screeching halt.

I was a few yards behind him and about to chase him across the street when I saw a police car at the intersection. The officer was staring at the tall, frightened Black man racing across the busy intersection without regard for his own or others' safety. The officer turned his emergency lights on and maneuvered his car into traffic to check out what was going on.

I froze at the corner of the intersection; certain the officer hadn't seen me.

The cars at the intersection remained parked as the police car made a U-turn and drove toward the crazed Black man running for his life. Once I saw that the police were pursuing him, I turned around and headed back to the student union building.

I wasn't surprised that Sidney was gone. Some people who had witnessed the weird scene were still there, and I was greeted with stares, whispers, and chuckles.

The incident became deeply disturbing the more I thought about it. I wondered what was going through Sidney's mind after witnessing such a bizarre scene. I resolved to tell no one about the fiasco, not even Jimmy, Darwin, or Daniel.

I was very concerned about losing my great relationship with Sidney. I was beginning to wonder if I had fallen in love with her. Everything clicked and fit when we were together. She was a head taller than me, and I loved it when she sometimes draped her arm across my shoulders as we walked. I knew she truly cared for me, and I could tell it when she kissed me.

The next day, I went to my classes. My last class was Calculus II. Unless we arranged something different, I would meet Sidney in our usual spot in the student union building. I arrived for our meeting. I stopped around a corner before walking into her view. I took a deep breath, turned the corner, and there she was. She looked up, and our eyes met as I walked toward her. My heart was beating in my throat. She suddenly burst out with roaring laughter. I was confused as I continued walking toward her.

She continued laughing when I reached the table and slowly slid down in the seat across from her. She looked at me with tears rolling down her face as she continued to laugh. I sat there. Everyone sitting around us stopped whatever they were doing and stared at Sidney. Sidney's uncontrollable laughter had become contagious as several people around us started snickering and laughing. It took a while for Sidney to bring herself under control, look at me, and not crack up laughing again. Finally, she said, "That was the most bizarre thing I have ever seen."

I said, "Please! Forgive me for doing that in front of you. I didn't do what it looked like. I pretended to do it. I was so angry at that fool that I had to do something, and I couldn't think of anything else; I was desperate. Are we okay? Will you continue being my tutor?"

She replied, "Yes, we're okay, as long as you're not planning on writing anything on my forehead!" Then she broke out into another uncontrollable fit of laughter.

"Great! Then can we try this again tomorrow?"

She stopped laughing long enough to say okay, and I got up to leave with her still laughing.

Sidney and I met for the next tutoring session and worked through a brief laughing spree. We continued to meet for the remainder of the semester. Our relationship was becoming more intense and serious. It grew as strong as it did because of the peaceful, quiet times we enjoyed together, especially at my mother's house.

Because of Sidney's tutoring, I was able to pull a B in Calculus II, and I had a 2.75 overall GPA. I saw the tall, lanky, Black basketball player around campus. He wouldn't say anything but glanced at me and moved on. I never heard a word about the incident from any of the other Black students on campus, so it appears the fool kept his mouth shut. I could understand it. How could anyone explain a crazy incident like that?

Little did I know that the last tutoring session with Sidney would be the last time I would see her. It was time to register for the 1971 Spring semester. I had not registered for school yet, and it looked like I wasn't going to. I truly didn't understand why. Something was stirring inside me; I was thinking about my dad, and I just didn't have the desire to be in school anymore. I also didn't want to tarnish all the hard work I had put in, so I waited until the end of the semester. Then, I dropped out of school and abandoned Sidney.

The 1970 fall semester was over, and Christmas was around the corner. I randomly thought about school and Sidney, but I was not returning and still didn't know why. I was also dropping the computer center job and working concert security at the Mini-Dome, where I saw Iron Butterfly, Linda Ronstadt, The 5th Dimension, Blood, Sweat & Tears, Richie Havens, It's a Beautiful Day, Ike and Tina Turner, and several other groups. From out of nowhere, I found myself praying, "Oh God, I don't want to disappoint my mother!" but the evil Mr. Hyde was constantly whispering to me.

A few months had passed, and one evening, I was sitting in my car sipping a half pint of Southern Comfort. I was deep in thought about my decision to quit school. Everything was perfect: my great relationship with my mother, my great relationship with Sidney, doing great in school, working the perfect job, but for some reason, I felt empty. There was a huge battle waging in my mind, heart and soul about Sidney, Jenny, and the baby. A huge weight of guilt was pulling me down because I thought I had fallen in love with Sidney.

I received several intimate signs from her that told me she had also fallen in love with me, but we never said it to each other, and yet, I was leaving Jenny and Anthony behind. My mental and emotional state was starting to shred apart even more. On May 2nd of 1970, I turned twenty, and two days later, college kids like me were killed at the Kent State massacre. And when Crosby, Stills, Nash, and Young brought out the song "Ohio," a whole different disturbance was dumped on my already troubled soul. I thought the war was supposed to be over there!

I was getting so depressed that I wanted to run away. Sly and the Family Stone song "Family Affair" echoed in my mind: "You can't leave 'cause your heart is there. But, sure, you can't stay 'cause you been somewhere else, you can't cry 'cause you'll look broke down, but you're crying anyway 'cause you're all broke down. It's a family affair." My mind was swirling in a storm about what to do about my "family affair," and I was allowing everything around me to crash and burn. I was feeling terribly depressed and broke down, and I just didn't want to deal with anything or anyone.

11

CHAOS AFTER COLLEGE

Between Heaven and Hell

New Year 1971 had come and gone, and not only was I missing school, but I was deeply saddened to learn that my brother was leaving Pocatello and moving to Seattle, Washington. First, I abandoned Sidney, and now I was losing my brother. Both were stabilizing forces for me. He asked if I wanted to take over his car, a 1968 Plymouth Barracuda 273 Commando V8. I told him yes, but I had no steady income to take over the payments. I had been thinking about my money situation since I was no longer in school and had no computer center job or grant money. I thought that instead of looking for a summer job at the Site, I should look into full-time employment. I stopped by to see Mrs. Purse, and she gave me a phone number to call.

The number was to human relations at the Site. I called, requested, and received an application; I filled it out and sent it back. A week later, I received a letter for an interview. I went to the Site for a whole day of interviews, and at the end of the day, I left with a full-time job working for the Atomic Energy Commission (AEC) in the Nuclear Fuel Accountability Group.

It was nothing but amazing. I had an opportunity for four jobs, but the job with the Accountability Group was the most interesting. It paid the most, and I started the following week, pending a secret clearance screening. I was not excited about getting up so early in the morning, but I was extremely excited to have landed such a great job so soon. It looked like Mrs. Purse had come through again.

I was able to take over the payments on the Barracuda and finally dump my beat-up 1958 Oldsmobile Super 88 (that I regretfully didn't take care of). I needed to celebrate my new job and new car, so I searched for Darwin or Daniel to share the good news with.

I thought that having a great job and driving a classic speedster would put me on the road to happiness, but how wrong I was. After working for about six months, I soon grew tired of getting up so early in the morning. It turned into a grind, with getting up at 5 a.m. to catch the bus at 6 a.m. Sometimes, I didn't get home until after 3 a.m., so I parked at the bus pickup, and someone would wake me when the bus arrived.

I gave a two-week notice before quitting. On my last day of work, I drove to work to leave immediately after being processed. I completed my exit processing and left Central with Jimi Hendrix blaring in my dust. I no longer had a job, and my concern shifted to paying for the Barracuda. I talked to my mom about my dilemma. Fortunately, a guy she was seeing named Harry wanted the car, so he paid off the balance. He wanted the car for transportation between Pocatello and the Clover Club potato farm where he worked. He would let me use the car when he came to Poky. Sometimes, he would let me keep the car during the week while he was working at the farm. We had an agreement that I would drive to the farm on Friday, pick him up, and bring him to Poky.

I was getting tired of not having a car at my fingertips. I still had some savings and could have bought a clunker to get around, but I wanted something nice after having the Barracuda for a while. Darwin and I drove by a car lot one day, and a 68 GTO caught my eye. It was the classic GTO green with a 350 Cubic Inch, 300 plus horses, and a three-speed automatic for $7,500. I made a deal for $5,000 down and financed the remaining $2,000 with a story that I was transitioning to a new job. I loved the GTO more than the Barracuda, and while the Barracuda was a nice, speedy car with the 273, my GTO would run circles around it.

It was well into 1971, and I had been out of school for a while. Things were getting busy and, unfortunately, getting busy in the wrong direction for me. My mom was extremely unhappy with me. I especially had one very bad incident with my mother at Bethel Baptist Church. I was walking home one Sunday morning since I left my car somewhere in Pocatello during the weekend. On my way home, I passed by the church. It was a beautiful day, and the church windows were open, and I could hear some hymns chiming from the windows. The music reminded me of my church choir days, and I felt like it was beckoning and calling me, so I made my way up the steep stairs. I opened the large door and stepped into a small lobby. My mom was the greeting usher, and when she heard the door open, she turned around, saw me, and stared at me in great surprise. She ushered me to a seat, and the entire congregation looked at me as if I were Lazareth, brought back from the dead. The music finished playing, and the pastor started his sermon, a message about Moses's faith and the Red Sea in Exodus 14. I suddenly recalled a lecture from my philosophy class, and I became extremely interested and excited, so while the pastor was delivering his message, I interrupted him with a question. My classy philosophy professor wore three-piece suits with colorful French cuff shirts, beautiful Paisley ties, and black high-top Converse All-Star tennis shoes. I used to think this guy was flat-out cool. One day, he delivered an interesting lecture from Exodus 14, centered around Moses and the Red Sea. The lecture stirred up more questions than answers, and I now understand that was the whole point of the lecture: to plant seeds of existentialistic concepts to question everything.

I caught the pastor off guard, and instead of him telling me to hold my question, he answered, and we started a short dialog. I was super curious and responded with more questions based on the philosophy class lecture. Soon, the pastor started to see the challenging nature of my questions, and he became extremely angry. He yelled at me and accused me of spouting abominations against God's Word and Christianity. He called me a heretic and told me to get out. My mother came up behind me, grabbed me by the ear, pulled me up out of my seat, steered me to the door, opened the door, pushed me out, and slammed the door shut. That was it. I was done with church and so-called Christians, and that was the last time I set foot in any church until the early nineties.

Deby, My Beautiful Rescuer

CHAPTER
12

DEBY, MY BEAUTIFUL RESCUER

She Was Always There

Jenny moved out of her uncle's house and moved in with her mother on 6th Street. One day, I stopped by the house to see Anthony. Jenny had left him with Ms. Bess., Ms. Bess was what I called her mom.

Anthony was lying in a rocker bassinet, crying uncontrollably with a baby bottle of partly curdled milk. He was in a dirty, crusty diaper, and only God knows how long he had been there. Ms. Bess was a 300 lbs., rocking chair-ridden lady. I wondered what would have happened if I had not stopped by. I didn't know what to do, so I left to locate a girl I knew named Deby. I was stressed about getting someone that I knew would care about helping my son, and Deby was my immediate choice. I located Deby and took her to the house, and she wrapped up Anthony and took him with us. She had me stop by a store for new bottles, formula, diapers, baby food, and baby clothes.

Deby was a gorgeous, young, mixed Mexican girl who sporadically dated me since 1967, but I had known her all her life due to the association of our parents.

I used to go hunting and fishing with my dad and her dad when I was younger. Our moms and dads would be together at gatherings at Ross Park, Cherry Springs, the Pools' house, or Uncle Bear Cat's place.

Deby was vastly different from other girls I dated in Pocatello. Jenny and Deby had a strained relationship because Jenny was still quite upset that we didn't get married, and she saw how close Deby and I were growing in our relationship, so Jenny always displayed glaring jealousy. We took Anthony to Deby's mom's house so she could care for him. Jenny eventually came by and picked up Anthony, but she was extremely angry and rude.

Jenny was still upset at me for taking Anthony from her mom's house, and one day, she violently attacked me. She caught me drunk at her older sister's house, we got into an argument, and she grew extremely angry, and out of nowhere, she hit me upside of my head with a bottle of ketchup, slicing open my scalp, eyebrow, nose, and top lip. I don't recall how I made it to the hospital. My mom was on duty when I got to the hospital, and she called the police. When the police arrived, my mom and the police wanted me to press charges against Jenny, but I wouldn't. I couldn't see my baby son's mother going to jail on felony assault and battery charges, even after her evil action.

Things only got worse with my drinking. I was drunk at an Idaho State High School basketball tournament at the ISU Mini-Dome. I was with Butch, a younger Black guy who was an All-State player when attending Poky High. I was arguing at the ticket booth that he should be allowed in free, and I got loud and obnoxious when some guy came busting out of a door next to the ticket booth. He rushed me, grabbed me by the collar of my jacket, yelled several racial obscenities at me, and hit me. I started swinging back on the dude. I soon outpunched him and beat him down to the floor. Suddenly, I was overtaken by two policemen who handcuffed me, threw me in the back of a police cruiser, and drove me to Bannock County Jail, where I was charged with drunken, disorderly conduct and assault and battery.

My neighbor, Mr. Stokes, bailed me out of jail. I eventually made it to court as my own lawyer. I pleaded innocent by self-defense with racial bias because of the racist names I was called. The judge kind of saw it my way, but since I incited the incident with my bad behavior—despite being attacked and battered first—I had to pay a fine and pay for the guy's medical expenses. The assault and battery charges were dropped.

One Friday evening, I was super buzzed. I walked into the Jim Dandy Club to hang out and buy a fried chicken dinner. The place was packed and busy, with one empty seat at the counter. I quickly grabbed it and ordered my food. I was listening to "Who's That Lady" by The Isley Brothers and washed down a bootleg whiskey with a wine cooler.

My old buddy Hayward was shooting pool and talking his usual trash. He lost his bet, so he reached into his pocket for money. When he pulled his hand out, bills of all denominations flew in the air and landed on the pool table and the floor. Everybody who picked up some money gave it back to Hayward except for a girl named Delores. Again, I was buzzed and didn't see her pick up any money. I also didn't remember her giving me any money, but she claimed she gave me some money to hold since she didn't have any pockets in the skintight outfit she had on.

The following week, I was at Big Alice's apartment. A group of us were sitting out front listening to music, drinking beer and mixed drinks. A car drove up and stopped in front of the apartment. Delores rushed out of the car, yelling and cussing at me. She walked toward me, asking about her money. I honestly didn't remember about the money she gave me. She pulled out a knife and started walking toward my GTO, threatening to cut her money's worth out of my car seats and cut me, too, if I got in her way.

I got up from the porch, went over to my car, and grabbed Delores. She turned on me and started coming at me with the knife. I was able to grab her, throw her to the ground, and disarm her. She got up and rushed at me time and time again. She was relentless. I finally threw her to the ground and hit her several times in self-defense. I didn't want to be so violent with a woman, but she was leaving me no choice.

As she was slowly rolling around on the ground, I got up and Alice told me to leave, so I jumped in my car and went over to Jimmy's house, where I stayed drinking for a couple of hours, and then I went home.

When I drove up to my mom's house, two police cars were parked out front, and an officer was talking to my mom. I parked my car, got out, and walked over to them. I told the police what happened, and they said they knew the details because Alice and other witnesses told them what happened; they even had Delores's knife. Delores filed a complaint against me. They said she was beaten so badly and taken to the hospital that they had no choice but to serve the complaint and arrest me.

At my arraignment of the assault and battery charges, the judge released me on my recognizance—OR—with a promise to show up on the set court date. He did this mainly because of the police report.

The court date came, and Delores didn't show, so the judge threw the case out. The judge gave me a stern warning. He told me that he didn't want to see me in his court again with another intoxication-related or assault and battery charge, or I would spend some serious time in county lockup.

I did have another drunken incident but with Jenny and not the law. I went to a house party with my oldest niece and her husband. I had several drinks before arriving at their house. When we arrived at the house party, I was feeling no pain and continued to party. Jenny was there, and she confronted me. I was too buzzed to understand what she was talking about, but we started arguing, and then she attacked me. We started fighting, and shortly after the fight started, several folks broke up the fight, and I left the party with my niece and nephew.

As we were driving, I started coughing up blood. Sometime during the struggle with Jenny, she stabbed me with an icepick. I blacked out on my way to the hospital. I woke up to what appeared to be an angel looking over me, not knowing I was under an oxygen tent in intensive care. As my head cleared, I realized the angel was a nurse. Then I saw my mother standing in one of her classic poses, her fists balled up and planted on her waistline. I was amazed that her glare didn't burn a hole through the thick plastic of the oxygen tent.

My mother said, "Well, she almost took you out with an icepick this time. Are you going to keep messing around with her until she finally kills you?" She turned and walked out the door.

I lay there thinking if Buddy Woods had left us alone, we probably would have got married, and this wouldn't be happening, or maybe not, since I wasn't ready for marriage. Wow! What a mess I'm in. Strangely enough, I found myself saying, *God, please help me.*

I was in the hospital for a couple of days. One day, my mom came to see me with the police. Again, they wanted me to press attempted murder charges against Jenny since she took the icepick with her with the intent to use it, but I couldn't do it.

Deby checked on me, and that made me feel extremely good. Evans came, and we played chess, and he told me how concerned he was for me. Jenny visited, and it scared the hell out of me—I thought she came to finish me off. She said she was sorry and started to cry, then we both cried. I soon recovered.

The Indian Warrior

I had been running shotgun for Jimmy and Darwin on some package deliveries and hitting the speakeasies a lot more. One evening, I was hanging out at Pete Morgan's, sitting at a table, eating some fried fish, collard greens, and a couple of slices of white bread, and drinking a cold beer. The front door opened, and an Indian man walked in. He was middle-aged, mid-sized, with a partial right arm missing below the elbow, and he walked with a limp.

It was the beginning of the month when the Indians received their money from the government due to their forced imprisonment at the nearby Fort Hall Indian Reservation. The Indian dude was drunk and was haggling with Pete over the price of a bottle of wine. He pulled his hand out of his pocket to pay, and a fist full of bills went flying in the air. I watched as the money fell to the floor. Pete and some other folks gathered bills of all denominations and returned them.

After seeing all the money, my mind clicked. Payday! I sat back and finished eating, just biding my time and waiting for the dude to leave so I could follow him, jump him, mug him, and take his money. After about an hour, he decided to leave. I didn't want to appear too obvious, so I sat back while he got up, put on his coat, and walked out the door.

I remained seated after he left, counting the seconds. I finally got up, said goodbye to Pete, and calmly walked out the door. Once out the door, I rushed into the middle of the street and looked both ways to locate the Indian. He was less than half a block away, going toward 4th Street, so I started trotting down the street to catch up with him.

When I got closer, I quickly ran up to him, grabbed him by the back of his jacket with my left hand, and with my right fist, I hit him hard in the back of the neck and head, thinking the blow would stun him and put him down. My blow didn't even faze him. He quickly spun around to my left. He suddenly grabbed me with his left hand, and with surprising strength, he pulled me in toward himself as I watched that right arm stub impale my chest. I immediately felt an excruciating, paralyzing pain. I saw stars as my knees buckled, and my body was sent into shock by the blow. I immediately realized that I'd made a serious mistake attacking this now one-armed Indian warrior! As tears started to form, my very next thought was in prayer: "God, please help me get the hell away from this dude, and *please* don't let this man hit me again!"

The one-armed warrior still had my left arm in a death grip, and with his stub weapon, he viciously pummeled me again and again. He tightened his vice grip on my left arm to a whole new level of pain. His nub of a weapon continued tormenting my chest, my shoulder, and my side as he hit me repeatedly with his evil weapon. Somehow, in my panicking struggle, I was able to turn to my right and start to pull away a bit. Due to the cold winter evening, a layer of black ice had formed on the road. I thought I could use it as a slim advantage since I had two good arms and legs. I frantically twisted and turned and pulled and jerked, and we both tumbled to the cold street.

As soon as we hit the street, I continued to twist and turn and ended up on my belly. His grip loosened on my arm so I could pull free, but now he had my coat sleeve—a small glimmer of hope. I began to claw the street with my fingertips, spinning and pushing and digging with the toes of my shoes as I struggled to escape with my life. I was able to free my arm. The pressure on the ski jacket zipper was too much and ripped open, allowing me to perform a metamorphosis and escape my polyester cocoon.

I worked my way out of the ski jacket, and fortunately, I wore a long-sleeved shirt. Suddenly, I felt another ungodly, excruciating pain in my left leg above my ankle. The warrior had released my jacket and latched onto my leg. His grip sent another paralyzing pain shooting through my body as I was consumed with terror again. I could no longer crawl, so I kicked the man's hand and arm. I started rolling and kicking until he finally let go of my leg. I rolled over on my belly and struggled to reach my feet on the slippery, icy road. I finally got to my feet and started making my way down the slippery street with my legs and feet churning like a cartoon character.

I began to thank God that I was finally free. When I finally got my footing on the slippery road, I turned my head to look, and the warrior was chasing after me. I screamed in horror and began running as fast as I could. I didn't turn around to look again until I was several blocks down Fremont Street, far away from Pete Morgan's and the Indian warrior.

My mom was right again, paraphrasing one of her frequently used bible verses, Galatians 6:7: "You will reap what you sow." That night, I learned a lifelong lesson about underestimating someone that I viewed as being weak. I learned my lesson, and that was the end of my mugging adventures.

The Drunk Tank

One day, I woke up in the Bannack County Jail's drunk tank. All I could think about was what the judge told me about appearing in front of him again with another intoxication-related or assault and battery charge, and I didn't even know why I got arrested.

I recalled being inside the bar, Charlie Brown's, when a brawl started outside, and someone came running inside yelling about a fight. I went outside and was suddenly defending myself, but I didn't know from whom. I remembered ducking, blocking, and then eventually throwing punches. Everything was a blur, and I ended up in a police car. The next morning, the deputies escorted everyone to the courthouse for arraignment. We were in handcuffs and ankle shackles, and we stood in a line in a waiting room. We slowly worked our way to the door that led out into the courtroom. I finally made it where one prisoner was ahead of me. When he was led out to the judge, I leaned forward and stuck my head out the door to see who the judge was. My heart sank and stopped beating, and I broke out in a cold sweat when I saw the judge who warned me not to show up in his court again. I still didn't know what the charges were, but I was sure assault and battery were on the list.

My case was called, and a county sheriff's deputy escorted me to stand before the judge. I stared at the floor as the court clerk read the charges: drunk and disorderly, assault, battery, and destruction of private property. As soon as I was asked, "What is your plea?" I dropped to my knees on the courtroom floor. Tears flowed, accompanied by slobbering and snot bubbles. I cried out to the judge, "Please don't send me to jail. I'm joining the service. Please don't put me in jail, Your Honor! Please!"

Two deputies came over and helped me back to my feet. To this day, I believe that my mom's prayers and the Grace of God influenced the judge to release me. I was instructed to bring back proof that I'd entered the service before the end of the court that day, or else a bench warrant for my arrest would be served. I returned to the jailhouse, went through the release process, and left the Bannack County Jail.

I gathered from the court proceedings that I got caught up in the police sweep due to the big brawl outside the bar. I could have easily avoided the arrest, but it looks like I was one of the idiots who was too messed up to run when the police arrived. In any case, it was great to be out of jail, but the thought of joining the service was frightening. I stopped by Ms. Bess's, who lived across the street from the jailhouse, and told her what was happening. She might have been a 300 lbs., wasting-away alcoholic, but she truly was a nice and wise woman. She looked at me and told me exactly what I needed to hear: "Well, I guess it's time for you to go."

My mom's house was a good distance from the jail, but I was able to make it there in no time. When I arrived, I was surprised to see my car sitting in front of the house. I walked into the house, and my mom asked, "So, were you in jail again?"

I didn't know what to say. I shrugged and replied, "Yeah, but I'm out and sorry."

Then she answered, "Well, you are headed for some big trouble, so you better do something and start with asking the Lord for help!"

Marine Corps Recruiter

Little did my mom truly know what was going on. I'd told the judge I was joining the service; my actual plan was to empty my bank account, fill my car with gas, and hit the road for Seattle. My brother told me I was welcome to come and stay with him, and he would help me to get on my feet.

I left my mom's house and got in my car. I sat there thinking about the judge and how he let me go because he trusted that I would do what I said I would do. My mind started to spin. I drove toward Yellowstone Road, where the Armed Forces Recruiting offices were. My mind was flashing between the judge and my mom—I truly didn't know what to do. In desperation, I cried out, "God, truly, I don't know about you, but please help me!" I wanted to run away, but my stomach turned sour when I thought about leaving, disappointing my mom and the judge, and abandoning Anthony like I abandoned Sydney.

I pulled up in front of the recruiting offices. I parked my car, and since I had thought of entering the Air Force after high school, I started there. I talked to the recruiter, but he wouldn't agree to return to court with me. The same occurred with the Navy and Army recruiters. So, I stood and stirred at my last option, the Marine Corps recruiter's door. A chill raced up my back as I thought about the war movies of fighting Marines I used to watch with my dad and the scary things I'd heard about the Marine Corps.

I entered the recruiter's office and said hello to a big Marine. He responded with a deep, growling voice, "Welcome, may I help you?" I thought about one of my older friends, a Marine Recon-Ranger who had returned from Vietnam, so I blurted out, "Yes, I want to be a Recon-Ranger, and I want to go to Vietnam and kill the Communists!"

He looked at me. "Well, I saw you when you drove up and parked. You first went to all the other recruiting offices and are now here. So, why don't you tell me why you are really here?" He invited me to sit down, and I told him the whole truth: I needed proof that I was going into the service or I was going to jail.

We started talking, and I was truthful about everything. I sensed he believed that I was telling the truth. Finally, he said, "Do you truly want to join the Marine Corps?"

I looked him straight in the eyes. "Yes, I truly want to join the Marine Corps."

The big gunnery sergeant asked me to call my mom to see if she was home. I called, and my mom answered the phone. We spoke briefly, and then I hung up. The Gunny got up from his chair, started closing the office, and we left. We got into his car. He drove a little way down Yellowstone, made a U-turn, then pulled up and stopped in front of a flower shop. The Gunny got out of the car and went into the flower shop. After a short while, he came out with a dozen beautiful red roses with white baby's breath and laid the flowers in the backseat.

He had the address, and he knew how to get to my mom's house on 9th Street, a few blocks from the recruiting office. We parked in front, exited the Gunny's car, and he retrieved the flowers from the backseat. We walked to the front door where the Gunny opened the screen door, knocked, and handed the flowers to me. My mother opened the door. The Gunny introduced himself and said, "Mrs. Vann, Presley has something he wants to tell you."

I was stunned. I turned to my mother and gave her the beautiful roses. "Mom, I'm joining the Marine Corps."

Mom started to cry, which started me to cry. We went into the house, stayed for a few minutes, and talked. Then, the Gunny and I returned to his car and headed to the courthouse.

We arrived at the courthouse and made our way to the courtroom. The Gunny motioned to a bailiff. The bailiff came over to the Gunny. They talked, and then the bailiff motioned for us to have a seat. The judge completed the proceedings with his current case, and then the bailiff went to the judge. They talked, and the judge looked up at the Gunny and me. The bailiff motioned for us to approach the podium. I could tell that the judge was a bit surprised by the expression on his face. He retrieved my case file, opened it, and told me that upon completing Marine Corps boot camp, any grievances will be dismissed, and my record would be expunged. With tears in my eyes, I told the judge, "Thank you very much, Your Honor, and I'm going to do this!"

The Gunny and I made it back to the car. We had a great conversation on the way back to the office. We parked and went inside, where we continued our conversation, and I signed some paperwork. He gave me a schedule of times and events for processing before I set off for boot camp. We walked to the door. I shook his hand and said, "Thank you for everything", and we gave each other a big manly hug.

I got in my car and sat there. Then I started to cry. Through my tears, I said, "Thank You, God!" What the judge had done for me was nothing less than a miracle.

13

A MORALLY IMPAIRED MAN JOINS THE MARINE CORPS

A Marine in the Making

I went to Boise Idaho for my service entry physical and testing before leaving for Marine Corps boot camp in San Diego, California. The electronics training with my father and a couple of years of college math paid off big time with the testing. Fortunately, I continued to practice my math even after leaving college. The times I stayed home and not out partying and acting like a fool, I would pull out my Calculus II book and worked and reworked Calculus problems.

The plane ride to San Diego was full of anxiety, flying into the unknown. Everything changed when the bus from the San Diego airport, transporting about thirty Marine recruits, rolled through the Marine Corps Recruiting Depot (MCRD) entrance. The bus stopped, and three of the most vicious-looking Marine Corps drill instructors (DIs) boarded the bus, yelling, snarling, and cursing, and rushed everyone off the bus. Once off, the DIs yelled, "Get your ass on the yellow footprints!" The scene was chaotic and reminded me of a disturbed anthill. All the recruits raced toward a pair of yellow footprints with a perfectly chiseled DI standing before us, shouting, "We don't care if you are White, Black, Brown, or Yellow. The only color here is Marine Corps green, and don't forget it."

The first night when the lights went out was incredibly quiet except for the roaming watch duty. I thought to myself, *"Oh! My God, what have I got myself into?"* I wanted to run away. These guys were the real deal, with their chiseled physiques poured into their crisp, tight-fitting uniforms. I lay in my rack thinking about Deby and could hear the song "Everything I Own" by Bread as I began to miss her so badly.

Marine Corps boot camp was very interesting. The food was surprisingly good, and everything was supremely organized. There was never a doubt about who was in complete control. It was drilled into us that the United States Marine Corps was first to fight, and our minds and bodies would be transformed into lethal weapons. The primary goal would be to learn how to shoot to kill and stay alive because every Marine is a rifleman first. We were indoctrinated to the understanding that war is not a bad thing; it is a necessary thing, and as Marines, we needed to master the "Art of War." By way of The Creed of a United States Marine, it was instilled in every Marine their rifle was everything revealed in part of the following creed:

This is my rifle. There are many like it, but this one is mine. My rifle is my best friend. It is my life. I must master it as I must master my life. Without me, my rifle is useless. Without my rifle, I am useless. I must fire my rifle true. I must shoot straighter than my enemy, who is trying to kill me. I must shoot him before he shoots me. I will...

Besides the Rifleman's Creed, we also had to learn the Marine Corps Hymn, the NATO phonetic alphabet, and the Articles of the Uniform Code of Military Justice. We spent hours learning and remembering tactical processes and procedures and how to march.

Shortly after the platoon picked up our rifles, I was commanded to come to the DI's office one evening and told to bring my rifle. My first rifle was an M14. It was in great shape with a beautiful walnut stock. I never thought about the weight of an M14 until that evening in the DI's office with the (PC) Platoon Commander and two DIs, a staff sergeant, and a sergeant.

The staff sergeant told me, "We've been watching you, and you think you're pretty tough, so let's see how tough you are."

Most of the troops in the platoon were between the ages of seventeen and nineteen, and there was a twenty-year-old. I was twenty-two. I was two years younger than my Platoon Commander, one year younger than the senior DI, and one year older than the junior DI, so I was an automatic target for the DIs.

I always thought that I was mentally tough with an unshakable will, but the prideful impression of myself was about to be severely tested. The DIs started attacking me with a synchronized, rotating, taunting process. They made me lean my back against the wall with extended arms, holding my M14, as I slowly stepped out until I reached a sitting position supported by the wall. I don't know how long I was in the position against the wall.

The DIs continued their attack on my manhood and mental toughness for what seemed like forever. Then they saw my toughness and realized that my will was about to shatter, so they stopped their little test. There was never a dull moment with competition drills against other platoons, precision marching, a rigorous obstacle course, force runs with our rifles, and training classes on martial arts, survival, small weapons, surveillance, and reconnaissance.

After a while, we headed to Camp Pendleton for infantry training and the rifle range, where I exchanged my M14 for a Mattel toy-looking M16. The night before we left for Pendleton, I lay on my rack, staring at the bottom of the rack above me. My mind was spinning about Deby, Sydney, Jenny and Anthony. Sydney was long gone, and Jenny turned evil, but Deby was always there for me. I lay there thinking I didn't even say goodbye to her when I left for boot camp. The song "Missing You" by Diana Ross kept ringing in my mind. I was ready to go to the rifle range, and maybe I could shoot some holes in my stupid reasoning for not saying goodbye to her.

Real Fire Power

The first training exercise was the disassembly and reassembly of the M16. Eventually, we had to complete the task in a certain amount of time or suffer through various physical corrective exercises. We also had to perform the M16 breakdown and reassemble in the dark. As the DI reminded us often, "War is a 24/7 business, and there are no timeouts for a soldier to clear a malfunctioning weapon in war!"

We finally made it to the rifle range, and I was excited for the opportunity to shoot. The Primary Marksmanship Instructors (PMIs) taught us B.R.A.S.S., which referred to Breathe, Relax, Aim,

Slack, and Squeeze the trigger. I reached my goal of becoming an Expert Rifleman when the shooting range was over. This meant I could shoot consistent, tight, center mass groups at a distance of three hundred yards with my M16.

The final week at Camp Pendleton came to an end. We loaded back onto the buses and headed back to MCRD San Diego. While on the bus to MCRD, I closed my eyes and thought about my mom, the recruiter, the judge, and how positive my "4-Crusaders" would be thinking of me.

My 4-Crusaders were four guys I grew up with in Pocatello. I became close friends with all of them, and I truly admired them. One guy I grew up with in The Triangle, two I met through Pocatello recreational sports, and one I met in junior high school, and these guys excelled in school and sports. They all were college graduates and became very successful teachers, lawyers, engineers, and businessmen while I was tripping over myself and stumbling through life. When I found myself in shameful and disappointing times throughout the decades, I would think of these four guys. Thinking of them during difficult times gave me pause and reflection, and my mind and conscience would start to drift toward a little clarity and allow for a splinter of light to shine through, and to possibly doing the right thing.

I really started to think about my mom. I accept that I didn't understand God, Jesus, and the Holy Spirit the way my mom did, but I wholeheartedly believed that her belief and faith was real and true. As I continued thinking about her, I started feeling extremely grateful, and once again, I found myself saying, "Thank you, God, thank you, Jesus, and thank you, Holy Spirit, for getting me this far!"

Ready to Be a Marine

It was the evening before graduation, and the DI announced everyone's MOS or Military Occupational Specialty. When he called out my MOS: 2853-Aviation Radio Repairman, he told the platoon, "Everybody, take notice. We have an Einstein in the room."

I beamed with a little pride as the DI finished calling everyone's MOS, and then we hit the rack.

I lay in my rack thinking about the boot camp misery, but I completely understood the reasoning behind it. It was a purging process that equipped Marines to stay alive. The DIs would say, "It's better to bleed a little in peace so you do not die during the war." Boot camp was tearing down a boy and building up a mean, green, fighting Marine.

Graduation day finally arrived, and I was so ready to leave. I wanted to get out of there, but there was a huge ceremony we had to go through. I made it through the lengthy ceremony, and since I had no family there, I grabbed my bags, jumped into a cab, and took off to the airport.

I was finally on my two-hour flight back to Pocatello. It was a free champagne flight, so after the plane was en route, I put down several glasses and felt no pain in a very short time. Before long, we landed in Pocatello. When I entered the terminal, I saw this tall, gorgeous creature looking at me, and I realized it was Deby. I was so buzzed that I forgot she was coming to pick me up. I was incredibly happy when I saw her. She always seemed to be there when I needed someone, and there she was, like a beautiful ray of life.

Marine Corps Graduation

Life Was Not the Same

Deby and I made it to my mom's house. We sat in her car and talked briefly, then hugged, kissed, and discussed hooking up later. I grabbed my duffle bag and walked to the front door. I knocked since I had no idea what had happened to my house key. My mom opened the door and was extremely happy and surprised to see me. I dropped my bag. We gave each other a big hug. She pushed me back and held me at arm's length. "What happened to your head?"

It must have been a shock seeing me with all my hair cut off, sporting my Marine Corps high-n-tight haircut.

I asked my mom about my car, and she said it got repossessed. I found out later that since I was paying for my car through an installment contract, my car could have been protected under the Soldier's and Sailor's Civil Relief Act of 1940. I didn't know about it, and the Gunny failed to inform me, so I lost my 1968 GTO.

I changed clothes. I didn't even go next door to see Anthony. I took off and hooked up with some of my boys. I joined them in burglarizing a stereo store, and I almost got caught by the police. A lot of my boot camp training got me through the police chase, and I finally arrived back home early the next morning. I discovered that I had a cut on the back of my leg from jumping over a chain-link fence, and it took a while to peel off the blood-soaked pants.

I was sitting in the moonlight on the back porch of my mom's house when it hit me. While, I was running, and hiding from the police, I was also praying and I realized that things were not the same; I had truly changed. Marine Corps boot camp had conditioned my mind to a whole different way of thinking, and I was in total denial about it. I tried to tell myself that nothing had changed and that I could just jump back in where I left off before boot camp, but how wrong I was. Then my 4-Crusaders flashed in my mind, and I know they would not have decided to do something so stupid.

I was home for two weeks, and before I realized it, I was on a flight from Pocatello to 29 Palms, California, to attend Marine Corps Communications Electronics School (C&E Schools). There was Deby again, this time driving me to the airport and again looking absolutely gorgeous. I felt very special that she was there to see me off, and I wondered if I would be able to hold onto her. We arrived at the airport, and I checked in my duffle bag. We had a short conversation and a goodbye kiss. I released her and started walking to board the plane. I turned around and looked back, and waved goodbye to her. My heart started to sink as I walked to the plane. I already started to miss her.

I reached my seat, sat down, and fastened my seatbelt. I closed my eyes, and they started to well up with tears. I was overcome with the most dreadful feeling of loneliness, now knowing I should have spent more time with Deby. Several songs started to play in my head, like "Oh Girl" by The Chi-Lites, "We've Only Just Begun" by The Carpenters, and "Let's Stay Together" by Al Green.

A Lonely Plane Ride

It was another free champagne flight, and I took full advantage of it. I was sitting alone, so there was no one to share my tears with, but the flight attendant noticed and asked me if I was all right. I love flying, especially the taking off, but none of that mattered as I continued drinking more champagne, trying to drown my sorrow. I truly believed that I had fallen in love with Deby. This was crazy because my life's theme songs had always been songs like "Ramblin' Gamblin' Man" by Bob Seger or "Hoochie Coochie Man" by Muddy Waters.

Another crazy thing about our relationship was that my mother really liked Deby. With any other girl I brought to my mom's house, she would give them a serious stare-down, making them extremely uncomfortable, and they would never want to return. This was with all girls—Black, White, Mexican, it didn't matter—but not Deby. So, now my new theme song was in the way of Elvin Bishop's "Fooled Around and Fell in Love," but it was different with Deby compared to how I'd felt with Jenny or Sidney.

Once I settled in on base, it didn't take long for me to get comfortable at the local bar, the "E-Club" or Enlisted Men's Club. Being twenty-two years old, I was of legal drinking age and also around the same age as several of my instructors, so I hung out with them. When I wasn't at school, I was pounding down beer and sneaking hard-liquor at the E-Club or some party in the desert. When I was with the instructors, they would encourage me to do better in school. They repeatedly reminded me that there still was a war going on and that I should be trying to qualify for all the schools I could go to and stay out of Vietnam.

Lunchtime rolled around, so I went to the instructor's lounge to hook up with some instructors and go to the E-Club. I was standing inside the instructor's lounge door and saw pictures posted on a message board. When they arrived, I asked, "So, are these honor students that graduated from the school?"

One of the instructors replied, "Yes, these are students that went to C&E Schools, and they're honored here because they went to Vietnam and didn't come back."

My whole being just froze. My mind became a vacuum. In a few moments, I started to recover from the shock of the reality of the war. I stood there staring at the pictures and started crying uncontrollably. My mind flooded with the young, dead Marines and then their mothers. My crying was barely under control when an instructor tried to console me as we left the lounge. He draped an arm across my shoulders and said, "If you want to honor those dead Marines, then do your part by making school your priority and not drinking and partying."

After that, everything about school seemed different.

A second major change was getting married. Barracks life was killing me, being associated with a bunch of teenagers 24/7. I discovered that a married Class-A brown-bagger could live off base. I called Deby and told her to arrange for our wedding. To this day, she constantly reminds me that I never proposed to her. We got married on Wednesday, February 17, 1973. I tried to arrange our wedding on St. Valentine's Day, the fourteenth, but the school's command would not grant me the leave.

Deby joined me in 29 Palms shortly after our wedding. Since I had so poorly planned everything, starting with no place to stay and not having a car, Deby returned to Pocatello. I graduated from school a few months later and returned to Poky.

Our Wedding Day

Another Lonely Plane Ride

After a short stay in Poky, Deby drove me to the airport on a cold November day. I loved wintertime in Pocatello, especially when it snowed. It often reminded me of Norman Rockwell's Christmas paintings and growing up in the fifties. But the thought of not being with my new wife for Christmas spoiled the whole Christmas mood. We arrived at the airport, and I checked in my duffle bag. We walked to my gate, and I held her for what seemed like forever, and then I gave her a goodbye kiss. My heart was so heavy as I made the lonely walk to the plane. After I got situated on the plane, all I could think about was going through a whole year without her, and the song "Precious and Few" by Climax echoed in my head.

It was a long flight, followed by a long bus ride to the base in Lakehurst, New Jersey. When I got to the receiving barracks, I was put in charge of the barrack floor, being the highest-ranking student. Now, I not only had to deal with the crude mentality of radiomen and wiremen, but I also had to deal with the unfamiliar parachute riggers and arresting gear operators. Lakehurst started as a very demanding place, having to deal with so many immature teenagers and the harsh winter weather. Wintertime was cold in Idaho, and the nights got pretty cold in 29 Palms, but the cold in New Jersey made both seem like summer vacation.

It was absolutely miserable. And since we were Marines on a Navy base, we had to display the ole Marine Corp grit. We were up at 5 a.m. on run day for a frigid three-mile run. At first, the early morning runs were miserable. The course cut through a wooded area saturated with trees, over low rolling hills, and a bridge spanning a frozen spring. The formation was led by a Marine sergeant who called a great bellowing cadence during the run. I eventually became consumed with the run and ended up enjoying it as time ticked away in Lakehurst.

The school days were long and tough but enjoyable. We learned to operate, calibrate, align, troubleshooting, and repair various aviation weather monitoring equipment and closed-circuit TV system. After school hours was a blend of camping out at the E-Club and excursions to the local towns of Bricktown or Lakewood but not Lakehurst. Even though Lakehurst was just outside the base gate, Lakehurst was off-limits to all military personnel because of bad public relations between base personnel and Lakehurst citizens. But this was even less of a concern to me because after what seemed like forever, graduation was upon us.

The day before we were dismissed from school, I was ordered to go to the Marine Corps school HQ office. My mind was in a tailspin as to why I was being summoned. I arrived, knocked, and was told to enter. The door was open, so I walked in and formally presented myself to a perfectly chiseled Marine Corps captain. Surprisingly, he had me remain at attention.

"Corporal Vann, are you aware of General Article 134?"

As my stomach turned, I replied, "Yes, sir, Article 134 is known as the catch-all article."

"Then tell me why you shouldn't be found guilty of Article 134 and held accountable for what was brought to my attention?"

He showed me a picture of my graduating class. There were seven Marines and six sailors. I was in the middle of seven seated Marines. I thought I had carefully concealed my extended middle finger, the "Bird." I had forgotten about making the stupid gesture, and no one noticed the visual anomaly when we were given our copies in class. I held the picture and looked up at the captain. Tears welled up in my eyes as I envisioned myself doomed by charges and office-hour proceedings.

"What the hell were you thinking, Marine? You deserve to be a lance corporal again and held back for office hours!"

My mind flashed back to court when my life was in the judge's hands. I almost dropped to my knees and started begging again, but I felt that would be inappropriate for a Marine. I stood there, scared to death, shaking, and thinking, *Oh God! Please help me!* Tears rolled down my cheeks. "Captain, please, sir, please forgive me. I am truly ashamed of myself; please forgive me!"

"Your leadership has been exemplary up to this point, and you should definitely be ashamed of yourself, Marine. This will be the first-class picture not displayed in the historical record of this school. Congratulations, Corporal. I hope you are truly proud of yourself. Now, get the hell out of here before I change my mind. Dismissed!"

I waited for the floor to open up and swallow me, and the captain yelled at me again. "Corporal, I said dismissed, or should something else happen here?"

"No, sir! Thank you, sir!" I did an about-face and jetted out of the office. I closed the door, walked a short distance, stopped, and leaned against the wall. I closed my eyes, and my mom, Deby, Anthony, the judge, and the Gunny recruiter all drifted through my mind. I was overwhelmed with shame. I finally gathered myself and left the building. And again, it looked like, by the Grace of God, I was heading back to California.

Exciting Plane Ride to California

After escaping potential doom in Lakehurst, I arrived at the 3rd Marine Air Wing El Toro air base and checked in at Wing HQ, then Squadron HQ, where I received my work and barracks assignments. I located and toured my workshop, and then I checked in at my barracks. It didn't take long for me to start off on the wrong foot as I made my way to the E-Club. It was a little after 6 p.m., and I hit it off with a Marine who had a car. We made our way to a friend's house in Santa Ana. We didn't arrive back at the barracks until after 2 a.m., and I was pretty messed up. But, the next morning, I got up, dressed, made it to the chow hall for breakfast, and made it to my shop before the 8 a.m. roll call.

This became my routine for about two months until Deby arrived. I had a great job as an Aviation Radio Repairman MOS 2853, maintaining a variety of radios, a cryptology unit, various weather monitoring equipment, and a vast closed-circuit TV network connecting the tower to all the flight squadrons on the base. The busy workload kept me from a nightlife of heavy drinking, smoking weed, and an occasional psychedelic. My recreational life took off in a great direction after I connected with one particular co-worker, a sergeant named Tom. He created a year-long training program where he taught me how to golf and play tennis, and we became very close friends.

Deby finally joined me, and we stayed in base housing for a week. Base housing assistance strongly recommended not living in certain areas, especially parts of Santa Ana. I didn't listen and picked an apartment complex in a tough Santa Ana area, saturated with Marines, around McFadden and Standard. The rent was cheap, and we didn't have a car, so I figured I would have no problem getting a ride to and from the base. We moved in late one evening. The next morning, we found out the kind of place we moved into. Because as we were moving in the back of the complex, a girl was being raped in the front of the complex.

I was in search of a ride to the base. The first door I knocked on, I interrupted two couples partying. Starting that night, we became close friends (we actually became lifelong friends) with Johnny and Terri and Pat and Grace, and from them, we were informed about the troubled apartment complex we moved into. First, a girl got raped, and shortly after we moved in, a low-life Marine stole our first brand-new color TV.

Within the time we were trying to prove he was the culprit, he got murdered, and we lost any chance to recover our TV. Next, we had a peeping tom problem, and I finally called the police. The officer who took the call, a former Marine, very discreetly suggested that, since I was a Marine and knew how to handle a gun, I should get a throw-away piece for protection due to the high crime rate in the area. I easily picked up a 32-caliber pistol with a taped handle and scrubbed the serial number. One night, I popped off a few rounds at the peeping tom, and that was the end of that problem.

After a few exciting months in Santa Ana, both of the couples we had grown close to moved not too far away to a town called Tustin. Not too long after they moved, they found us an apartment, and we were thrilled to get out of Santa Ana.

In October of 1974, I re-enlisted for six years, was promoted from corporal (E4) to sergeant (E5), and received a $16,000 re-enlistment bonus. Deby and I were finally able to buy a car. We financed a brand-new 1974 Toyota Corolla, and our lives went to a whole new level.

My time at El Toro was almost like having a regular job. But Deby was not only plagued with my excessive drinking and drugging, but she now also had to deal with my tennis tournaments, golfing, and basketball league. Plus, when I would arrive back at the apartment complex, there was always a group of people in the recreation area playing music, cooking, shooting pool, playing basketball, drinking, and getting high. Then, we would plunge into the pool around 1 a.m. before going to our apartments and hitting the sack.

Fortunately, Deby had made several friends, and when winter rolled around, she only had to contend with my work schedule and the basketball league. Still, my excessive drinking and drugging were escalating. I was having the time of my life, and I thought everything was going great. Then, one day, Deby told me she was pregnant.

Life Back in the Desert

Our first daughter, Carmella, was born on June 11, 1975. Before Deby's delivery date, we attended several (LaPlace) birthing classes, but I was absent during Carmella's delivery. My not being there would haunt me for a long time.

My mom came to California after Carmella was born, and it was great having her visit. But her visit was also emotionally and morally convicting because I was not living as she expected. Plus, I knew she would sternly disapprove of how I was treating Deby, especially now with the addition of her first grandchild. My mom stayed with us for three weeks, and Deby was extremely happy to have her there. Even though Lillie Vann was not Deby's bio-mother, she was a great, comforting mother to her. One of the first things my mom asked was, "Are you reading your bible?"

I shook my head, ashamed.

"Where are you going to church?"

Once again, I gave her a familiar blank, dumb look.

I missed my mom after she left, and I knew Deby definitely missed her. Soon after she left, I picked up orders to return to 29 Palms for radio technician school in April of 1976. My current MOS was Aviation Radio Repairman (2851). The school could be up to a year long if I completed the first part to become an aviation radio technician (2866) and then the second part to qualify to become an Aviation Communication Systems Technician (5939).

Carmella was almost a year old when we arrived at 29 Palms. I had rented half of a duplex on Sunnyslope Road off the 29 Palms Highway, about five miles from the base. Deby and Carmella could have stayed in Tustin, and I could have commuted on the weekends, but again, I didn't want to deal with barracks life and the associated duties.

School was great, with more advanced electronics, analog signal processing, radio theory, and detailed radio repair down to the component level. We connected with a large Samoan community because I played tennis with two Samoan students in my class. This was when we learned that Carmella had a special adaptability to languages. Carmella was a little over a year old and was picking up the Samoan language.

I also grew close to a Black gunny sergeant, who was one of my systems instructors and who also played tennis. Gunny had a Japanese wife and two beautiful little girls, four and six years old. His wife and girls embraced Deby and Carmella as much as the Samoans did, and in a short time, Carmella was picking up Japanese. Gunny and I would play tennis after school and then go to his house to enjoy great Japanese food and very little drinking. Gunny was a great man and a great influence.

School and life were going great in 29 Palms, but there was a dark side. I met a couple of instructors and civilians who traveled on the forbidden trails of the Stomps. Frequently, I used my tennis as a cover while strolling in the dark corridors with these folks. One of the civilians was a former Marine who lived in the desert, and he was a major drug dealer. Much like TC back in Pocatello, this guy dealt in large quantities of everything, including cocaine and heroin.

I got to know this guy through Dave, one of the civilians I played tennis with. Dave used to race motorcycles across the desert until one particular race. Instead of maneuvering completely around a big tumbleweed, he rode too close and crashed into a boulder. The accident ended his promising career, and due to years of recovery, he got hooked on pain meds along the way.

Dave would pick me up on Saturday or Sunday mornings to play tennis. After tennis, we would take off to "The Place" in the desert. The first time Dave took me there, we were held off by a rifle pointing out the front door. After the dude recognized Dave, we were allowed to enter.

Pete was a big, bearded, soft-spoken, half-White, and half-Mexican dude. His house had a bland Adobe-style exterior but a nicely decorated interior. Dave had previously mentioned me to Pete, who offered us a seat. "I hear you're from Pocatello, Idaho. Idaho is a nice state. I have relatives there. How can I help you fellows?"

Dave said, "We would like to pick up an ounce and a couple of hits of Mescaline if that's okay?"

Pete stared at us for a moment. Then he got up, disappeared down a hallway, and returned with the goods. He handed them to Dave and offered each of us a beer.

Pete was a likable and intelligent dude. In the Marine Corps, he had attended C & E schools for radar training. Later, he became an instructor assistant and stayed in the Stomps at the end of his tours. Dave and I downed the Mescaline with our beers, hung around for a while, then psychedelicized our way to Palm Springs for a couple of hours, then Dave eventually dropped me at home.

The Toyota was gone, which made me feel a lot better. I figured Deby and Carmella were off enjoying themselves with someone who truly appreciated them. I had always felt great that everyone took to Deby and Carmella, who was a beautiful little girl. The care people displayed for my wife and daughter helped me cope with my feelings of shame and disgust. But I continued to sink deeper and deeper into my depressive behavior thanks to Mr. Hyde's selfish influence.

A year passed, school ended, and we were in the process of returning to El Toro. The day before we were to leave, I went out to Pete's place to hang out and score. A party was going on, but it was actually a big drug transaction gathering. Even though I was allowed to stay, I felt extremely nervous being there, so I decided to leave. I said goodbye, got in my car, and drove back down the winding road to the stop sign before turning onto 29 Palms Highway.

I looked across the highway and saw several police cars that appeared to be staging for something. The moment reminded me of an evening in Pocatello when I walked out of Juck's and saw the police surrounding the bar. Mysteriously, I was allowed to get into my car and drive away. Same thing this time. I was allowed to turn onto 29 Palms Highway, and as soon as I turned, the police cars took off down the road toward Pete's house, and I went on my merry way. It was like they were waiting for me to leave before they jumped into action. I immediately thought about my mother and her Grace of God thing.

Deby and I finished packing up the car and took off back to El Toro. I remember driving from the base, and as soon we were headed down 29 Palms Highway, my mind started playing back the tape: "My Life and Times in The Stomps." The movie was a mix of mixed emotional scenes: scenes of the beautiful desert, scenes of pleasant times on base, scenes with the mighty Samoan community and the gunny's family, scenes of struggling and then finally succeeding in school, and scenes playing tennis, but very few scenes of the three of us enjoying family life together.

A gloomy cloud of booze and drugs drifted in and covered any wholesome light of what could have been a great tour with my family. I loved being in the desert; this could have been a different experience if I hadn't had such a need to dwell in the darkness. It was so entrenched in me to lounge in the gutter and to wallow in the mire, keeping Mr. Hyde company. It was much like being back in Pocatello and satisfying my soul's requirement to be hanging out at the speakeasies.

Leaving for Okinawa

Once back at El Toro, we settled into our new apartment, but I would no longer have my great job with the Base Communications Squadron. With my MOS changed to (2866) aviation radio technician, I was assigned to the Marine Air Support Squadron 3 (MASS-3) and given orders to go to Okinawa.

Shortly after settling in with all the newness, Deby and Carmella drove me to Edwards Air Force Base. It was suddenly déjà vu, like in Pocatello, when Deby drove me to the airport en route to boot camp, electronics school in 29 Palms, again in New Jersey, and now, once again, we were saying goodbye.

I was awakened from a deep sleep by the pilot's announcement that we were about to land at Tokyo Haneda Airport and then on to our final destination, Naha Airport in Okinawa. After landing in Okinawa, I was shuffling toward the front exit of the plane, and I had no idea what was in store for me. As I got closer to the door, I could see the air changing from the cool air conditioning in the cabin to hazy, foggy air. I finally reached the exit, and on my first step outside of the plane, I walked into a horrible environment of hot, liquid air. I couldn't breathe, and I was instantly soaked in sweat. I was in a state of shock, and I thought I was going to die on the spot. I started crying, but it didn't matter because you couldn't tell my tears from the sweat`.

I wobbled a bit as I started to step down, and two flight attendants noticed I was having some difficulty. They immediately rushed to my side and grabbed my arms to steady me. I said in my mind, "Suck it up, meathead, you're supposed to be a Marine!" so I quickly gathered myself and I thanked the flight attendants. Walking down the steps from the plane, I supported myself on the handrail; my mind flooded with, "What have I got myself into this time? Am I going to survive this?"

I finally arrived at MCAS Futenma in Ginowan City and eventually made my way to the NCO barracks. The next step was to the E-Club, which became my sanctuary outside work and the barracks.

I was assigned to the Marine Air Support Squadron 2 (MASS-2). The shop was very busy with a gunnery sergeant and several staff sergeants, sergeants, and corporals, but there was not a lance corporal or private in sight. I worked in the ground-to-air communication section that consisted of several radio and maintenance vans. Even though the Vietnam War was over, I was still in the front yard of the real Marine Corps and the war zone. El Toro was a picnic compared to Okinawa, where workdays could range between ten to fourteen hours days, depending upon the required support for a variety of deployments.

I had been on base for about two months, and I had to come to terms with my drinking and partying or dying in the miserable, humid environment. I thought about what my mother would say to me and what my 4-Crusaders would do. They were all about doing the right thing. So, I stopped drinking, smoking, partying, and making Sake runs to Old Town Okinawa with some old-timers. It was tough, but I eventually worked myself into great mental and physical condition.

One day, I was informed that everyone was going on the mother of all deployments called Galant Eagle. It was a massive war game involving the US, Japan, Southeast Asia allies, and Australia. This exercise was huge. The day following the major deployment announcement, I was promoted to staff sergeant (E6) and ordered to pack up and head off to my first Navy ship—a Landing Ship Tank known as the USS Schenectady (LST-1185). After a week of ocean maneuvers, we dropped anchor on the Philippine Island of Mindanao for three weeks. The island was amazingly beautiful, with spectacular white sandy beaches, crystal clear ocean water, abundant wildlife, and a close encounter with a huge king cobra snake. I befriended some Filipino locals and traded blank paper, pencils, empty C-Rations cans, spare clothes, and an empty gas can for a handmade butterfly knife, a bolo knife, and a buffalo ride. It was amazing how nothing went to waste with the Filipino people.

Before long, we were back on the LST and headed for the Navy base at Subic Bay, and we docked at Olongapo City. Due to the horror stories, I'd heard about Olongapo City, I only toured the town during the day with some Motor-T guys who knew their way around, but I spent the night back aboard the ship. Days later, our LST finally docked at White Beach back in Okinawa. I was back on weekend liberty at the huge Kadena Air Force Base recording room, where I recorded some great soul and soft rock music.

I was fortunate to catch a military flight back to the States for Christmas. It was great to spend Christmas week at home and not be overcome with a fog of drunkenness. Too soon, I was heading back to Okinawa. Once back on The Rock, a little depression set in until one day, I met a master sergeant and a Black gunnery sergeant from

MACS-4, a unit across the runway from my unit. They came to our shop to borrow some UHF radio parts, and I was assigned to help them. In a short time, the Gunny and I forged a great friendship (a friendship that continues to this very day).

I only had a week before rotating back to the States, and the racist gunny in charge of the shop assigned me to secured carrier duty to Korea, and I defied the order. He filed charges against me, and I filed discrimination charges against him. We were ordered to report to the group lieutenant colonel. After I told my story to the colonel, he strongly advised both of us to drop our charges and come to terms with each other, or else things would quickly escape our control. So, we agreed to drop the charges and part ways. I caught the Gunny totally off guard with my counter-discrimination charges. The colonel did not want any racial controversy in his group, along with all the race issues in Okinawa at the time.

Before long, I was walking through the terminal at Edwards Air Force Base back in California. I was thrilled to be back home finally, and the two most beautiful ladies in the world were there to pick me up. During our walk to the car, I thought about the strenuous year behind me. Then, for some reason, I started thinking about my mother, and then, out of nowhere, I found myself saying, "Thank you, Lord."

CHAPTER

14

A MORALLY IMPAIRED MARINE LEAVES THE MARINE CORPS

Leaving the Marine Corps

The year I spent in Okinawa gave me a great glimpse of what the real Marine Corps was like. Initially, the heat and the humidity made it a literal hell, but I made a choice not to fight it, and I stopped smoking and excessively drinking. Plus, despite the extreme environmental conditions, I got in great physical shape. The year was enjoyable, but I was thrilled to go home.

Returning home, I was a well-adjusted man, husband, and Marine. Life was cruising along great until I went to the wrong party at Mike's house. Mike was an older Marine I used to work for at El Toro. The party was at his big house, with plenty of great food and alcohol. I started slowly with a beer, stepped up to a couple of glasses of wine, and eventually graduated to various mixed drinks. I didn't remember driving home that night. Mike's house, unfortunately, became a frequent watering hole since I had an open invitation to visit any time. Pretty soon, more liquor was at our apartment, and it was steady drinking when I visited any of the neighbors' apartments. When I played tennis, there were wine coolers and beer instead of water or Gatorade in my cooler. I also started making frequent stops at several neighborhood bars, especially Newport 5, where they made the best Long Island Iced Tea.

I eventually hooked back up with the Black Gunny from Okinawa, and we would consume large quantities of Rum and Coke while listening to sixties soul music. The Gunny and the Top arranged my transfer to their shop in Wing Station Communication Squadron, and I was thrilled with the transfer. The boozer fog was growing around me, but I enjoyed the electronic work at the new shop, and Top Etch was huge in helping me advance my electronic knowledge.

The junior troops were all very pleasant and intelligent corporals and sergeants, so I didn't have to worry about or deal with much immaturity. Unfortunately, there were a couple of junior troops potheads with whom I grew close. Even though a highly unmilitary relationship existed between me and some subordinates, everyone remained focused on doing their job correctly while respecting rank and work priority.

Me and junior troops

I also dealt with a very unpleasant Marine Corps officer in our section captain who was in charge of all the electronic shops. This guy was a pure paradox. He was an old-core maverick type with his Hitler-looking mustache. He was built solid as a rock with vice-grip hands. He was an alcoholic's alcoholic who picked up his officer commission during the Vietnam War. However, with respect to his age and time in service, he should have been at least a lite bird (lieutenant) colonel, but again, he was a drunken bum of an officer. The guy was an ass, and everybody feared him with his forceful, intimidating personality. The guy was also very intelligent, but I didn't allow him to push me around with his abrasive, verbose, and crude behavior. I was never insubordinate toward him, but I let him know that I respected the Marine Corps officer rank but had no respect for the man behind it.

Things deteriorated so badly between the captain and me that by the time I was leaving the Corps, he initiated office-hour proceedings against me. The guy was so angry at me because I would not cower at his every word and rude gesture, and he hated it when I would greet him, "Hello, Cap!"

One day, we were summoned to the colonel's office, much like what had occurred between me and the Gunny in Okinawa. But this time, the colonel knew that my complaint about the captain's crude personality would probably go against him, so he squashed the whole situation in his office. Fortunately, the captain respected the colonel and agreed to drop the proceedings. We apologized to each other and shook hands, but the captain left with revenge in his alcoholic, pickled mind and mud hole of a heart.

I had reached the start of my ninety days of terminal leave. I was still in the Marine Corps, but I wouldn't be required to come to the base. At the end of the ninety days, I would return to the base, go through the checkout process, and finally be rid of the captain.

But the captain got his day of reckoning with me. The day I checked out, I had to go to the captain's office to sign my exit papers. There was a section party that particular day, so I made my way to the party at the picnic grounds. The captain was in his familiar drunken stupor. I carefully approached him, and he told me to come closer. I had to be careful because he was a judo expert, an All-Armed Forces Judo Champion, and quick as a cat, and I didn't want to be grabbed. I inched closer, and before I knew it, he grabbed my wrist. A chill rushed through my body as he twisted my arm and soon had me on the ground. He maneuvered me into an excruciatingly painful hold. He was talking trash as he contorted and twisted my body. I didn't say a word, although I wanted to cry, but I was not giving him the satisfaction. Finally, a Master Sergeant spoke out and told the captain I'd had enough, and the captain finally let me go.

I was in terrible pain as I slowly picked myself up off the ground. I held back all my emotions as I picked up my papers. "Sir, will you please sign these?"

The captain snatched the papers and pen,

walked over to a picnic table, signed the papers, and left them on the table. I walked over to the table and picked up my papers and pen. I walked down the walkway, leaving the picnic area, and turned toward the captain. "Thanks for nothing, Cap!"

Hearing the mockery in my voice, he rushed toward me. Several Marines grabbed and restrained him as he wrestled, yelled, and cursed at me.

I smiled and waved. "Goodbye, Old Cap!"

I had been in the Marine Corps for eight years and wanted to re-enlist for six more years, but Marine Corps Headquarters would not let me change my current critical MOS to a different critical MOS, so I got upset and decided to leave. I left an E7 promotion, a 5939 MOS change, and a $30,000 reenlistment bonus on the table, but I didn't care.

When I left the base for the last time, I stopped at a bar down the road from the front gate. My mind was oscillating between cheerfulness and sorrow, and it continued with mixed emotions until enough booze drowned out all hope for any sensible reasoning. In the end, Deby had to come to the bar around 10 p.m. to pick up her extremely drunk husband.

Life Outside the Green Machine

I got a job during my terminal leave. A civilian radio electronics consultant informed me of a company named Baytron Systems. This was great since daughter number two was born at the beginning of the year. My interview was a breeze since I would be working on the same radios I'd worked on in the Marine Corps. I spent my last year in the Corps boning up on computers because that's what I wanted to do eventually. Baytron refurbished radios, radars, and several minicomputers, so I'm hoping I can take advantage of the computer section.

I talked to an engineer in the computer section who told me about a local company called Basic-4 Computers. I went to Basic-4 and breezed through another interview. I had no practical digital experience, but based on my book knowledge, testing equipment experience, and gift for gab, I was hired. This is where I learned about digital electronics. I learned synchronous computer design concepts, micro-coding, Basic and C programming languages, and how to use the golden digital tool, a 32-bit logic analyzer. It was 1981. I'd been out of the Corps for about a year and was working at the Basic-4 R&D campus in Tustin, not too far from the apartment.

Within a couple of months, I was transferred to a huge repair facility in Santa Ana, and this is where my life took a brutal turn. I organized it, and then I was put in charge of a new section that worked on mini-computer boards. I had four to five technicians working for me, and several of them were hardcore party animals. We had a couple of wall lockers, located at discreet locations, stocked with booze, weed, and coke in the huge facility. Probably 75 percent of the workforce was current or prior military, so it was much like in the Marine Corps. People worked hard and prioritized completing the task and preparing to play hard at the end of the workday.

In 1982, I worked at the Santa Ana facility for over a year, and daughter number three was born; then self-created tragedy struck. A parts clerk left an expensive part for me to pick up since I had procurement authorization. Earlier that day, we created a fake parts requisition form for the part, and later, the form was supposed to be collected before the end of the workday and destroyed. I picked up the part and signed the fake parts requisition form. Later on, I met up with everyone at a bar and delivered the part. We collected and split the funds and continued to party. I got up late the next morning since I hadn't returned home until early the night before. The phone rang as I was getting ready.

A co-worker told me I probably shouldn't come in because the police were there waiting for me. They had the paperwork I signed, which was supposed to be collected and destroyed. I immediately collapsed to the floor and thought about my mother, and I could hear her paraphrasing one of her bible verses, Luke 8:17, again, "What's done in the dark will come out in the light."

Instead of going to the Santa Ana Police Station, I went to work. When I arrived, I went to my manager's office, where two police detectives immediately arrested me. I was handcuffed and paraded out of the huge warehouse in front of a large crowd. I was placed in the back of a police car, and I thought, *Oh my God, what have I done?*

My eyes were closed, but tears were flowing as I sat handcuffed in the back of the police cruiser. I pictured my mother in my mind and how she would be so disappointed in me for jeopardizing my family. I pictured Deby and the girls in my mind when I would have to shamefully face them. I pictured my recruiter and the judge. I pictured my 4-Crusaders and how they wouldn't so easily trash their integrity as I had. I wanted a black hole to open up and suck me into endless nothingness.

Given A Second Chance

I not only lost the world's most perfect job, but I lost it in a most humiliating way. All of the hard work I'd put into learning this great, new profession, and I threw it away due to booze, drugs, and bonehead Mr. Hyde thinking, but fortunately, my friend Mike showed up and bailed me out of jail.

A month passed, and it looked like my mom's Grace of God suddenly appeared. I received a phone call from the corporate human relations director inviting me to a lawyer's office for a meeting. In the meeting, I was told that all the charges against me had been dropped, and an apology was extended to me for how I was treated. I would receive retro compensation, and my bail would be refunded. It was nothing less than a miracle that left me bewildered.

I was extremely happy that the miracle was a huge relief. I couldn't imagine what was going through Deby's mind when her whole world crumbled because of her husband's stupid, selfish, reckless, boneheaded behavior. I received generous compensation, so I wasn't worried about money for a while. Another great part of the miracle was that no criminal charges were filed, so I still had a clean police record and a future in the computer industry in Orange County.

I immediately created a list of ten favorable computer companies from the Sunday Orange County job listings. I researched and refined the list to five companies from the list of ten. I created a résumé, went to the five companies, filled out an application, and left a copy of my resume. Three companies responded, and I liked Western Digital Corporation the most. I focused on WD because the manager who interviewed me was former Air Force. He expressed a sincere desire for me to work for him. I accepted his offer and went home to tell Deby the good news.

I started working for WD in October of 1984, located off Von Karman Street in Irvine. The new job timing was perfect because daughter number four was born in 1985. In 1990, WD moved from Von Karman to Irvine Spectrum, and I convinced some engineering friends to leave Basic-4 and come over to WD. Once they joined WD, I received hiring bonuses between $2,000 and $3,000 for each of their engineering levels. This only further financed my escalating drinking and drugging problems.

Down the road company layoffs were occurring, and usually, there was a company-wide announcement, but not this time. People were blindsided by their exit announcements, and stress was extremely high. One day, I was called to our manager's office. My heart stopped, I stopped breathing, my palms were sweating, and I went to the bathroom thinking I was going to throw up.

Our manager was a really sharp young guy. When I walked into his office, he was direct and cold. "I heard you know how to use an emulator, so you can go to the Test Engineering group or go to your cube, pack up your stuff, and wait for security to escort you to the lab to pack up and then escort you to Admin."

The guy was heartless in how he talked to me. Since I chose Test Engineering, he blandly told me to report to the Test Engineering manager. The meeting with my manager was extremely disturbing, and it gave me an excuse to go to my car and hold a counseling session with the booze and the white lie I had in the glove box.

I felt the meeting was shocking and stressful, and I allowed it to springboard me into escalating my drinking, and more drugs came along for the ride. I usually saved my indulgence for lunchtime and after work, but I was starting to slip out of my car during work hours, drinking and snorting a line or two. The truth be known, I was in total denial that I was heading into serious trouble. I started taking longer lunches and sometimes wouldn't even return to work. I could hide a lot of my missed time because my job required me to go to several floors of the fifteen-story building for meetings, training, and helping with various projects, but things were starting to get really bad for me.

Twice, I regained consciousness after passing out in my lab. I came to and found myself sitting on the floor, leaning against a workbench. Fortunately, I was by myself both times I passed out. I'm sure I passed out from a cocaine overdose. My heart was still racing; I had the world's worst headache and a terrible, nasty taste in my mouth, and it was a real struggle for me to open my eyes. I would try to stand up, but my knees were weak and wobbling as I reached out for anything I could get my hands on to help me rise to my feet before someone entered the lab. I was confused after the first time I recovered from one of the episodes, but the second time scared me to death. I couldn't tell anyone about what was going on. I needed help, but all I could say was, "God, please help me!" the desperate plea came about, not knowing if God could or would help me.

While at work, I was suffering the side effects from my Dr. Jekyll and Mr. Hyde conflicting personality struggle. Dr. Jekyll was the team player and the engineer, but Mr. Hyde was the devious, conniving, drunken, drug-laden idiot.

I thought about what my mother used to say about the heart of King David. She would remind me that, regardless of all the bad things he had done—deceit, adultery, and murder—he still maintained a heart for God. He eventually repented, and that was the basis for God forgiving and blessing him. I would wonder, in my foggy, drunken, druggy state of mind, if God could see me in my misery the way he saw King David in his. I had no one to turn to, so all I could do was call on God for help. But as I wondered if He could help me, I had already planned to go to my car for another glove box counseling session, and this was the insanity I found myself trapped in.

CHAPTER

15

AT THE END OF MY ROAD

A Day Filled with Warnings

It was a Friday before noon, and I emailed a report to my manager summarizing my successful testing on my project. I left my lab on the twelfth floor, walked to the elevator, pushed the lobby button, and waited for the doors to open. When the elevator doors opened, I stepped in, pushed the lobby button, and walked to the back of the elevator as the elevator started its descent. In my excitement over the successful testing of my project, I grabbed the rail on the back wall of the elevator and vigorously shook it. Then I heard the elevator wind down to a halt, and the fault lamp started flashing on the utility panel.

I opened the utility panel, picked up the phone, and reported being stuck between the twelfth and tenth floors. Forty-five minutes later, the elevator started running again. While waiting in the elevator, I checked my wallet and had $800. I needed $1,000 to purchase the amount of rock I wanted, so I got off the elevator and started canvassing specific coworkers starting on the tenth floor, down to the second floor, and I borrowed the remaining $200.

Earlier that day, I'd called my dealer, Raja, who was married with two little kids. Her husband, Ray, was a nice guy, and was in the Marine Corps. He and I got along very well. But the poor guy was strung out from Raja's dealing. Raja's street smarts enabled her to navigate through the dangerous drug dealing world in which she thrived. Her toughness helped her to survive through being cheated, robbed, and raped. Yet she continued because she was caught up in the same white lie I was caught up in.

Our first meeting was at a mutual dealer's apartment in Tustin with a guy named Leonard. This guy was an extremely strange and interesting Filipino dude. One time, I went to his apartment, and he wasn't home. His wife invited me in, so I took a seat where I had a full view of the living room. Leonard suddenly appeared out of nowhere. He didn't come down the stairs or through a doorway. He just showed up. Another time I went to his apartment, and I joined in on a weird ritual with a small group of druggies. Everyone was high, but he asked for someone to lie on the floor, and the rest of us sat in a circle around them. Those of us in the circle held hands and started repeating a chant. As we continued the chant, he had us place our hands under the person lying in the circle and slowly lift the person's body.

Another time, I was alone with Leonard when he looked at me and told me where I had just come from and where I was headed upon leaving. In both cases, he was correct. On another occasion, he got up and motioned for me to follow him. We walked outside, and he told me to be still and listen. It was so quiet. Not even the birds weren't chirping. Then he said, "Here it is." In a moment, an earthquake occurred.

The final time I was with him in his apartment, out of nowhere, he suddenly told me I should leave. I instantly became startled, so I rushed out to my car, jumped in, and started driving to the exit. I stopped at the driveway and started to turn onto the street when several police cars suddenly turned up in the driveway. I just knew in my soul they were headed for Leonard's. I thought about another one of the bible verses my mother paraphrased: Psalm 37:27: "And boy, you better run away from evil." I never saw Leonard again after I left his apartment that afternoon.

Once I collected the funds I needed, I took off to my car. When I got to my car, I realized I had left my keys in my lab. I rushed back into the building, and the elevator crawled back up to my lab, and I grabbed my keys. The elevator crawled back down to the lobby; I rushed out to my car, sped out of the parking lot, and raced onto the 405 North freeway. It was just before noon, and the freeway was a bumper-to-bumper mobile parking lot. It took me over half an hour to get to the MacArthur exit. Then I hit practically every red light going down MacArthur to Harbor. Once on Harbor, I hit every red light as I made my way to the Holidee's Motel, where Raja lived. The motel's parking lot was full of flashing red lights with police and emergency vehicles, so for over an hour, I waited at the McDonald's across the street.

I started to think, here I am again, another setback—the elevator, my keys, the 405 mobile parking lot, red lights all the way here, and now this emergency mess. I began to wonder what was going on. Then, an image of my mom filled my mind, followed by an image of Deby and the girls. Then, my 4-Crusaders strolled through my mind, and I started to feel a little troubled and uneasy. I was starting to have second thoughts. But Mr. Hyde started defending the white lie, drowning out every wholesome thought of me, changing my mind. All I could think about was loading my pipe and taking a hit.

Finally, the police and all the emergency vehicles left the motel's parking lot. I rushed over and parked in front of Raja's apartment. I hooked up with Raja, and we took off to a dangerous apartment complex called the Firehouse—it sat behind a real fire station on Harbor. In the apartments, doorways were cut in the walls between the individual apartments, so you could stand at the first apartment and almost look through to the opposite end apartment. This dealer house knew Raja well, so we were allowed to enter the first apartment. There wasn't enough rock available where we were, so we were told to go through to the next apartment, where the rock was being cooked and packaged.

The journey through the apartments was disgusting. There were people having sex, women nursing babies, little kids running about, someone sitting on a toilet with no door, scantily dressed young teenage girls sitting about, cats and dogs roaming around, trash and clutter strewn about, and a variety of unpleasant odors lingering in the air. I knew for sure that my 4-Crusaders wouldn't be caught dead there, but there I was, yielding to the call of the white lie.

We eventually made our way to the cooking area. There were several card tables with women cooking over electric hot plates surrounded by boxes of baking soda, pots, and jars. On a bigger table was a huge quantity of processed rock packed in glass vials and small plastic bags. We scored and returned to the Holidee's and away from that heavily depressing place.

We made it back to the motel, and we sat at a table in the small dining area. I laid a large rock on the table and pulled out my pipe as Raja and Ray pulled out their pipes. The pipes are better known as crack pipes. They are made of about six inches of glass tubing with a bubble cooling reservoir in the middle and a smoking bowl at one end that is filled with a small screen first, then some copper mesh. A small piece of rock is placed on the mesh, lit with a lighter, and a deceitful love affair begins while inhaling at the other end.

As soon as we started to party, someone knocked on the door. Ray answered the door, and it was another one of Raja's customers. Raja got up and staggered to the door, then went to the couch, got her coat, and put it on and said to us, "I'll be back."

When Raja left, I packed up all my stuff, and I took off to a head shop on Euclid to pick up new pipes, screens, lighters, and copper mesh. While driving, my mom drifted into my mind, and Deby and the kids wavered through, followed by my 4-Crusaders. I was filled with an immense sense of disappointment, but the desire for the white lie derailed my thoughts and kept pushing me on.

I arrived back at the motel before Raja, so Ray and I set up the new pipes. Then, Ray had an idea: when Raja returned, he would smash her old pipe against the wall. After she freaked out a bit, he would give her the new pipe, and we all would have a great laugh and continue to get high, and I agreed to the stupid idea.

We were smoking another rock when Raja returned. She took her coat off, put it on the couch, and sat down with us. Ray took her pipe piece, and he acted like he was passing it to her but instead pulled it back and smashed it against the wall. Raja's eyes grew huge. Her mouth dropped open as her caramel-colored complexion turned pale. Ray laughed as I reached into the bag for her new pipe. Raja got up and walked away from the table into the kitchen. Suddenly, she came running out of the kitchen with a huge carving knife that looked like an Arabian sword.

She was screaming like a crazed woman as she charged Ray with the huge knife. As she thrust the knife at Ray, he caught her by the wrist. Ray's chair toppled over backward, and they hit the floor. I jumped up, grabbed the bag of rock, my pipe, and a lighter, and tossed everything into the paper sack from the head shop. I grabbed my coat and a bottle of E.J.'s brandy I had brought in earlier. I ran to the door as they continued to wrestle on the floor. I rushed out, jumped into my van, and tossed the sack in the passenger seat. I wrestled my coat on, started the van, and hastily exited the motel parking lot.

It was about 3 a.m. Saturday morning on February 20, 1993, when I started driving back down Harbor. I was traumatized thinking about Ray and Raja rolling around on the floor with the huge knife. My mind was flooded and straining with all kinds of thoughts and emotions, but one question was pounding in my head: *What's going to happen with their children?* I felt that question would forever haunt me, especially after I saw them standing in the bedroom doorway as I rushed out of the apartment. My heart was throbbing with immense sadness for the two little kids. I felt like two more victims caught up in the wake of my destructive behavior. I was so tired, and all of the strange delays of the day started to press upon my mind, and I began to wonder what was going to happen to me.

I Called Out to God, and He Heard Me

I was beginning to feel my life was a yoyo and oscillating between bad and worse. Strangely enough, the Grace of God thing my mother repeatedly told me about continued to show up in my life, time and time again, and enabled me to escape some tragic situations. But this time, when God's Grace showed up, it directed me to an AA meeting.

It was about 4 a.m. that Saturday morning, and I had been away from home since Friday morning. I found myself sitting in the manager's parking stall at the apartment complex where we used to live. I reached over to the passenger seat and grabbed a sack containing the bottle of E.J.'s brandy. I unscrewed the lid and had a big drink. It burned its way down as I screwed the lid back on and tossed it back in the seat. I sat behind the wheel, trying not to think about Ray, Raja, and their children.

I moved from the driver's seat to the back of the van. I pulled out my last Marine Corps wool blanket and spread it over the van floor. I picked up my portable cassette tape player and loaded it with Jimi Hendrix's "Are You Experienced" tape. I hit the play button, and the song "Manic Depression" immediately flooded my mind. As Jimi was jamming, I reached up in the front seat, grabbed the sack, and emptied it on the blanket. I took the golf-ball-size piece of rock cocaine and broke off a generous chunk, placed it in the pipe bowl, flicked the Bic, put the flame to the bowl, and took a big hit.

I felt weirdly disturbed after the big hit, so I dropped the pipe and turned Jimi off. I leaned back against the side of the van as my 4-Crusaders flashed in my mind, thinking they wouldn't be in this predicament. A vision of my mom popped into my mind, and I could hear the 23rd Psalm echo in my head.

In desperation, I cried out, "God, please help me! Jesus, what am I supposed to do?" The van instantly filled with a strange, soft glow as my mind milted into perfect clearness. I felt God knew that in my heart, I had truly hit bottom and surrendered everything. He poured out His love, grace, mercy onto me, and instantaneously, He supernaturally healed me, and I slowly gathered myself in His peace.

I was completely sober-minded, and it was the greatest sensation ever! I dropped down on my hands and knees and gathered up the rock of cocaine, the pipe, the bottle of E.J.'s, the cassette tape player with Jimi, and I rolled it all up in the blanket. I opened the van's sliding door, walked over to a nearby Dipsey dumpster, raised the lid, and threw everything away.

I got back in the van and sat behind the wheel. I felt like I was floating in space, and I was bewildered about what to do next, but I didn't want to do anything to spoil the wonderful feeling and mental clarity. Then I suddenly thought about Rich. He was the apartment complex manager who also used to be one of my dealers.

About a year earlier, I approached Rich to score some goodies. Much to my amazement, he said, "I don't deal or get high anymore."

"What happened?" I asked.

"I stopped doing all that. I don't drink anymore, and I'm going to AA."

Recalling what he'd said, I jumped out of the van, rushed out of the parking stall, and ran to a narrow walkway between the back of the parking stalls and the back wall of a complex to his bedroom window.

I knocked on the window.

Rich bellowed out, "Who the hell is it? I've got a gun, and I'm going to shoot you if you don't get the hell out of here!"

So as not to get shot, I called out, "Rich, it's me, Presley. Where is that 6 a.m. AA meeting you attend?"

There was a long pause. Then he said, "Meet me around front."

I went to the front of his apartment, opened the gate, and walked into his patio area. Rich was standing at the patio door opening with a little smile on his face.

"Will you take me to that 6 a.m. meeting?" I asked.

"I don't attend that meeting anymore. It was too damn early in the morning, but it's at the church across the street from Foothill High School."

"Come on and go with me?"

"Naa, you'll be okay. Let me know how it turns out." He turned away, wearing a bigger smile, and closed the patio door behind him.

I turned and walked back to the van. I jumped in and drove out of the complex. I turned right on Newport and drove toward Dodge Street. I turned down Dodge Street and drove slowly in front of the church. I drove down a little further and made the U-turn. I pulled over, parked in front of the church, and sat in the van.

Suddenly, two men were standing at my passenger door. One knocked on the window and said, "Turn off your van. You're in the right place."

I got out of the van and walked to the curb. One of the guys stuck his hand out and helped me to the sidewalk, and they introduced themselves. Two or three other meeting members came over, patted me on the back, and said hello. They all walked into the meeting with me, and it was great how welcomed they made me feel! We walked into the church recreation room. The meeting was called to order shortly after we entered.

We went through all the meeting's opening formalities, and then it came to the time to share. I didn't necessarily want to share, but they asked me if I would like to share, especially since I was the new kid on the block. That particular meeting was called an old-timers meeting. They usually didn't get a lot of new folks, but I suddenly showed up and became a bit of a novelty. I tried to describe the last couple of days and explain what happened to me in the van, as I searched for words. Still, everyone sat and listened.

At the end of the meeting, I received a Big Book and a 12-Step and 12-Traditions Book. I was invited to return with the 90/90 challenge—90 meetings in 90 days. I later discovered several bets were made on me not to show up the next day or last the week and bets I wouldn't last the month.

A group of guys escorted me out to my van. I drove away as the group stood on the sidewalk, waving goodbye. It was amazing. I had never before in my life experienced anything like what had occurred. I felt that I was truly headed in the right direction, but headed where I didn't know.

I drove home, and when I arrived, I parked, rushed out of the van, and ran to the front door. I opened the door and saw my four beautiful daughters sitting on the couch. They were dressed up like they were ready to go somewhere. Their pretty little faces simultaneously turned toward me with their gleaming brown eyes fixed on me. I closed the door behind me, and Deby appeared seemingly very angry.

She stuck her hand out and growled, "Give me the keys!"

I noticed luggage sitting at the end of the couch. She packed clothes for herself and the girls, and they were about to head out the door. She'd finally had enough. I had pushed her to her limit.

I pleaded with her to go to the bedroom and talk to me, but she snatched the keys from my hand and walked toward their luggage. I gently grabbed her arm, pleading for her to talk with me.

She snatched her arm from my grip, turned to face me, and glared. She looked at our daughters. "Stay here. I will be right back." I followed her to the bedroom.

I shared a condensed summary of my morning. I explained how I'd cried out to God and asked Jesus what to do, and something hit me, rendering me sober instantly.

She stared at me like I was crazy.

I continued, explaining that I'd come from an AA meeting and showed her my books to prove it. Then, I gently took her hand and pleaded with her not to leave. I assured her that something had happened, though I couldn't explain it. Nonetheless, something big had changed. I begged her for one more chance.

She stared at me, long and hard. I believe she, too, must have felt something had changed in me. But all she said was, "We'll see."

We returned to the girls in the living room. I could see they sensed a change in their mother. She told them they could go, so they slowly got up and went to their bedrooms. As they left, I saw a little confusion on their faces, but they left joyfully. I think they were happy they weren't going anywhere.

I returned to the bedroom to take a shower. As I sat on the bed, a happy vision of my mother entered my mind, and I was filled with tremendous joy. I wished she was there to see that something wonderful and powerful had happened to me. I truly believe that being an old-school Holy Spirit warrior, she would see and understand a deeper spiritual meaning behind what had occurred. I finished my shower, dressed, and left the bedroom with my AA books in hand. Walking down the hall, I looked into the girls' two bedrooms. I momentarily stood at each doorway and gazed at my beautiful little girls, and they all returned warm smiles.

I sat at the dining table with books as Deby continuously gave me nervous looks. Finally, she shouted, "Well, are we still going?"

I had no idea what she was talking about.

Turning to me, she growled. "Are we still going to Riverside?"

Then I remembered. We had plans to go to Riverside to watch the Greg Haugen and Julio Cesar Chavez fight. Her question was an invitation to join them.

I glanced at the clock. It was 5 p.m., and the fight started at eight. "Yes!" I said.

We got the girls ready, packed up the van, and took off to Riverside. As we drove, I thought about how much my consumption of booze and cocaine had increased over the last five years. I was slowly losing my memory, my eyesight, and my mind while suffering from endless insomnia. I was scared to death and feeling hopeless. Until that day, I did not believe I could stop drinking. I thought I was destined to yield to the white lie and eventually maybe die.

We arrived at Jess and Lib's, and the party was in full swing. We were greeted with offers of beer, booze, smoke, and lines, but I turned down everything. I had no desire to drink or get high and disturb the wonderful way I was feeling. Instead, I sat in the living room and enjoyed watching the fight.

At one point, Tia—"Yo-Yo"—approached me. "You want a beer or something to drink?" I said no, and she stared at me and said, "What the hell is wrong with you?"

I told her, "Things have changed." She stared at me a little longer, then walked away.

We stayed until the end of the fight; then we headed back to Orange County. I was driving with a clear mind, and I never felt so alive. While driving, I began giving a deep-hearted thanks to God, and yet I still didn't understand Him. I also gave sincere thanks to my 4-Crusaders for providing me with periodic cognitive references of integrity. They would flash in my mind as wholesome character examples for me to reflect upon and helped me to ponder about simply doing the right thing. With my whole heart, I thanked my mom for planting the biblical and spiritual seeds that allowed God's Grace to flourish about me and provide ways for me to escape Mr. Hydes' destructive influence.

16

GOD'S SPIRIT LED ME TO AA

Start Step 3 *(Finding God—His Will and Not Mine)*

It was 5 a.m. on a Sunday, and I was preparing for my second AA meeting. I jumped out of bed from my first night of full, peaceful sleep in a very long time. What happened was nothing less than a miracle, and I still couldn't explain it, but my mind was no longer in a constant fog.

I continued attending the 6 a.m. meeting. The early morning drive was a pure joy ride, and I appreciated everyone's sincere morning greetings. I was becoming more comfortable, so I started sharing more often and searching for a sponsor. I decided to ask a guy who frequented the meeting. He was not one of the set-your-clock-by attendees, but I liked him. I asked him to sponsor me, and he appeared slightly surprised but agreed. He was a former professional of some type, I think a doctor or a lawyer. He was very intelligent with my twisted sense of humor, and he was very approachable. I felt comfortable talking to him, and he truly engaged with me when we met for Big Book and 12-Step sessions.

Everything was going well with the meetings and my sponsor until one day, we were supposed to meet for a 12-step study, and he didn't show. I left after a two-hour wait. I repeatedly called him, but no answer. It had been almost two weeks, and I had still not heard from him. I went to a noon Brown Baggers meeting, and I found out he was dead. I heard he was found in a motel where he had been drinking and died from alcohol poisoning.

This threw me into a huge, confusing psycho frenzy. Here I was, thinking that this dude, who appeared to be a seasoned, sober AA member, was going to help me stay sober. Wow! I was so depressed about my sponsor's death that I almost dropped out of AA. Suddenly, all the pre-and post-meeting prayers didn't mean a thing to me, and all the sharing was a bunch of people lying through their teeth. When I left that meeting, I imagined everyone driving away, reaching underneath their car seats and pulling out a bottle of booze. But, for some reason, I stayed with the program. A lot of it had to do with reaching the 90/90 milestone. I was determined to get through it and show that I was the real deal.

Soon, I was a little over four months in AA. I continued to attend meetings in a very mentally hollow state, and it was reflected in my sharing. I received responses from several people like, "What the heck are you talking about?" I never spoke directly about the death, so it was understandable that people were confused about my sharing. Several people expressed concern that I sounded like I was on the verge of slipping—all except for one old-timer.

After a morning meeting, an older Jewish guy walked up to me, laughing. He put his hand on my shoulder and said, "So, you're looking for a sponsor?" This blew my mind because it was like he was reading my mind. I looked at him and said yes. Still laughing, he said, "Okay, come on, let's go."

As we walked to the parking lot, I said to him, "You know, my first sponsor drank himself to death, and I don't know how to handle that."

He put his husky arm around my shoulders, and he said to me, "Well, you don't come to AA to get sober; you come to AA to get help, and some people can help you, and some people can't, so you just keep working on your program." Suddenly, I was okay, and all the anxiety that had become a huge burden melted away.

My new sponsor's name was Doug. Our first meeting was at Benjie's NY Deli restaurant in Santa Ana. I told him that my first sponsor and I had completed Steps 1 and 2, but I couldn't move on until I completed Step 3 and came to an understanding of what God's will was for me. I constantly shared about it, and I talked to numerous people, but no one had an answer. He told me I was making it too complicated, as most folks do. He said that most people are looking for some big theological answer, but it's amazingly simple: if you want to know what God's will is for you, all you have to do is ask Him.

His simple answer threw me for a loop! I said, "What?"

He repeated that people make things too complicated. All they have to do is ask God, "What is it You want me to do?" He said some people call it prayer, but all you have to do is be honest and talk to God.

Doug asked, "Where did you drink?"

I told him that I used to drink everywhere: at home. I'd hide booze throughout the house and drink it while sitting on the toilet, in the bathroom shaving, in the garage, at several bars, and at work. I had booze in the glove box and beer, wine, and liquor in a cooler in my car trunk. I even had booze and drugs stashed at different places around town.

He said, "Then that's where you must also talk to God. Be honest and talk to Him while sitting behind the wheel of your car, at work, or on the toilet. You talk to Him wherever you are, wherever you go, but you first thank Him for being sober that day, then ask Him to forgive for all the harm you've done and ask Him what He wants you to do." He emphasized, "Be honest, keep it simple, give Him thanks, then talk to Him about what's on your mind and your heart." He added that as a destructive alcoholic, lost in the new world of sobriety, I should continuously say, "God, thank you, and please forgive me, and please help me," being a recovering alcoholic in a foreign place and not knowing what to do.

Doug told me that AA is a platform for sobriety. It's a process, and the process is funneled through a 12-Step recovery program. Having a sound program is everything to the recovering alcoholic. He repeated a quote I'll always remember: "It works if you work it, and it won't if you don't." He said the 12-Step Recovery Program has more than twelve things to do. The recovery process includes prioritized actions carried out in twelve steps. Some steps stand alone, and some steps work together. He laid out a simple description for me:

Step 1 Admit You Have a Problem (Stand-alone)

Step 2 Get Help Greater Than Yourself (Stand-alone)

Step 3 Find God (Stand-alone)

Step 4 Clean House— *Write about the alcoholic you* (Works with Step 5)

Step 5 Clean House— *Talk about the alcoholic you (* Works with Step 4)

Step 6 Move On— *Become Willing to ask God for help* (Works with Step 7)

Step 7 Moving On— *Becoming Humble to ask God for healing* (Works with Step 6)

Step 8 Making Amends— *Who did you harm* (Works with Step 9)

Step 9 Making Amends— *Who do you approach that you harmed* (Works with Step 8)

Step 10 Daily Accountability (Stand-alone)

Step 11 Draw Closer to God (Stand-alone)

Step 12 Give Back— *This Step Never Ends!* (Keep giving back)

On to Step 4 *(Cleaning House—my fearless moral inventory)*

I met Doug at the restaurant to plan my fearless moral inventory. I was to examine my past and document how my defects resulted in actions that affected and harmed others. I was told to get a notebook and write down everything from my past I could remember. I was instructed to be as specific as possible with names, places, and dates, and if I couldn't remember a name, place, or date, to leave a blank space to fill in later but to write down *everything*. I would later come to understand that this was an important purging process. I started my fearless moral inventory with some of the more destructive incidents in my life:

The Indian Girl

Early one Saturday morning, I was cruising down Lander Street, driving past the Jim Dandy Club. Jimi Hendrix was jamming on my eight-track tape player as I was chasing vodka shots with Boone's Farm Strawberry, smoking a joint, cruising slowly, and looking for something to get into. I saw three heads peeking around the corner of a building. I stopped the car and turned the headlights off. Two men ran across the street, and they disappeared around the building where bootlegger Paralee lived.

Then, I saw a female poke her head around the corner of the building. I slowly drifted down the road until I got to the corner of the building. I stopped, and she came into view. I waved my wine bottle and the joint out the window and asked her to come and party. She walked up to my car window, and we started talking. She was a nice-looking Indian girl. I asked her to get in the car, and she looked at me and got ready to get in my car. Then she changed her mind and started backing away.

I opened my door, got out, and started walking toward her. She continued backing up, so I reached out and grabbed her by the arm. She started pulling away as we wrestled to the back of my car, and then she slipped and fell to the pavement. I reached down to pick her up, and suddenly, bright lights lit up everything, followed by flashing red lights. It was the police!

Two police officers got out of their cruiser and walked toward us. The girl was squirming on the ground, and I turned to the police and said, "I was driving down the road, and she was lying out in the street. I got out to help her."

One of the officers turned to me and said, "Okay, we'll take it from here. You can leave."

I got back in my car and drove away.

I continued partying for the remainder of the weekend, and I finally made my way to my mom's house and crashed. My mom arrived home from her nurse's aide position at St. Anthony Hospital about 10 a.m. Monday morning. My mom finished making breakfast, and I sat down to eat with her. My mom often talked about things that occurred during her shift, like when an overweight gentleman was overlooked. They found a bedpan that had been stuck to his bottom for an extended time, and his fat butt cheeks had filled in the bedpan, and it was quite an ordeal to get it off him.

She said, "They brought in a young Indian girl that hung herself in the county jail."

Suddenly, my heart felt like it stopped beating, and I stopped breathing. I felt lightheaded, and I grew numb and empty and ready to throw up. I just knew it was her.

The 12-Step Book highlights an alcoholic's crazy and damaging conduct and where we made the invention of alibis a fine art. I wanted to tell my mom about the Indian girl but couldn't say anything. My heart was so heavy. I sank into a deep sadness, and I felt miserable. I wanted to crawl out of my skin and separate myself from the wretched fool who possibly caused the tragedy. But I was stuck with Mr. Hyde's miserable decision. I finally went to the bathroom and threw up.

Old Man Robertson

My father died on Wednesday, November 18, 1965. A little over a year later, my mom started dating a guy from Denver, Colorado. Everyone called him Mr. Robertson, a skillful licensed mason. He was a stout, highly intelligent, clean-looking older dude who knew how to lay on the charm.

One Sunday afternoon, he was at my mom's house pouring on the charm/ I didn't trust him. He asked me if I wanted a job. It was summertime, and I was looking for work before I started working at the Site. I told him yes. He wrote down an address and told me to meet him on Monday at 6 a.m.

Early Monday morning, I drove to the storefront on the north end of town where we were supposed to work. I became the hod carrier, the mixer, the brick carrier, and the clean-up; I did everything. Old Man Robertson didn't do anything but lay brick. The storefront covered three stores in a mini–strip mall. It might not sound like much, but it was a lot of work for a sixteen-year-old. Old Man Robertson didn't care. He was mean, hard, tough, and relentless.

I worked from 6 a.m. to 6 p.m., and again, I did everything. I brought my lunch, but sometimes, he made me work during lunch while he took off. When I did something he didn't like, he would push me, yell at me, call me names, and taunt me about quitting. If I complained about anything, he yelled at me and called me insulting names.

At the end of the week, we completed the job. I finished all the clean-up at about 5 p.m. He told me he would be at my mom's about 7 p.m. because he was taking her to dinner. I got home, cleaned up, and waited for him to arrive. Normally, every day after work, I would come home and crash and not even shower because I was so tired. I was also tired that Saturday, but I showered because it was payday, and my anxiety was in overdrive. I couldn't have cared less about being tired.

Old Man Robertson showed up at seven. He walked through the door and didn't say a word to me. He stared at me and growled, "What do you want?"

I said, "I'm waiting to be paid."

Suddenly, he rushed at me, grabbed me by my shirt collar, and slammed me against the wall. He continued growling at me. "What's wrong? You think I'm not going to pay you, you little bastard?"

I didn't know what to say. He took out $135, and with the money clenched in his fist, he hit me hard in my chest. It hurt and stunned me. I took the money, walked out the door, got in my car, and drove away.

I drove to my niece's house. Her husband was a pipefitter, and I knew Rob would know if I deserved more money. I got to their house in the midst of a party. I pulled Rob aside and told him my story.

He said, "Man! You got robbed! That job was probably worth at least $3000 to $4,000, and you should have been paid hundreds of dollars for all that work." I was very upset!

I stayed and partied for a while, then I returned to my mom's house and discovered that Old Man Robertson had dropped her off. I knew where he was going and headed down to Lander Street. I drove around until I spotted his car parked behind a bar. I parked a little down the alley, got out, and walked to the bar's door. I peeked in and saw he was partying. I ran back to my car and pulled a hammer from the trunk.

I rushed to his car, smashed the passenger side window, unlocked the door, and entered. I felt under the front seat and found a .38 pistol. I opened the glove box, searched it, and found a paper bag containing $300. I called it a fruitful evening, ran to my car, got in, and drove away.

The next day, I told my mom about Old Man Robertson and how he had cheated me and taken advantage of me. I also told her that I had gone down the way to find him and located him in a bar with a woman and another couple, getting drunk. I asked my mom not to see him or to allow him to come to the house anymore. She agreed. I'd gotten the old dude out of my mom's life. Now, I would step up my game and make his life miserable.

One day, I drove by Payton Place, where he stayed in a single-bedroom apartment at the top of the stairs. His car was gone, so I took a pry bar and went to his apartment door. I easily pried open the front door, walked in, searched around, and found $600, and then I left.

Another time, I went searching for Old Man Robertson, and I drove by Payton Place, where his car was parked out front. I parked down the street, reached into my glove box, and took out a small, sharp skinning knife. I made my way to his car and jammed the knife close to the wheel rim and air stem on all four tires. I made my way back to my car and drove away. A few days later, I saw his car running again with four new tires in the parking lot of a popular restaurant. I parked my car close to his, grabbed the knife again, ran to his car, and stabbed all four tires the same as before. A week later, I saw his car, with four used tires, parked in front of another bar. I carefully sneaked over to his car and crawled under the rear of the big Buick. I tied a tow rope that I had in the trunk of my car to his rear axial and a street sign. I took off and returned about an hour later. There he was, with the police, a crowd, and the street sign ripped away from the curb.

I heard talk around town about Old Man Robertson talking to everybody about what was happening; word was that he had become a bundle of nerves. I saw him. He was no longer the sharp-looking old man with his mohair hats, pressed shirts, slacks, and shiny shoes. He looked like a bum. One Saturday evening, about 10 p.m., I drove by the Jim Dandy Club, and there he was, coming out of the Club with an Indian woman and a sack of food. He was sloppy drunk as he opened the car door and flopped behind the wheel. The Indian woman staggered to the passenger side and plopped into the passenger seat. I followed them to Payton Place. They staggered out of the car, and it took them forever to get up the stairs, so I decided to leave and return later. At about 2:00 a.m., I grabbed the pry bar, went to his door, and broke into the apartment. I heard heavy snoring coming from the bedroom, so I immediately went to work searching for money. I found a bunch of cash. I filled two pillowcases with cans and jars of coins that took an extra trip to the car.

I wanted to make a statement, so I went back and gathered their clothes and shoes, and all the towels, sheets, blankets, pillows, toilet paper, paper towels, curtains, and anything that wouldn't make any noise and tossed it out the bathroom window to the alley below. I grabbed the pry bar and took off to my car. In the car, I counted a little over $700 in cash, and I saved the change to count later and drove away.

The following week, I saw Old Man Robertson driving down the street looking like an empty, broken old man. A couple of weeks later, I heard he left town. Some of his relatives came, got him, and took him back to Denver. When I heard the news, I felt a little sad for him for some strange reason. My mother would be so disappointed in me if she knew I was the one who drove the old dude crazy and eventually out of town. I could hear her paraphrasing a verse like Exodus 14:14, "You let the Lord fight your battles!"

Well, I certainly didn't do that.

The Unreverent J. D. Harris

It was near the end of 1966, a little past a year after my father passed away, and I was still missing him greatly. My mom settled all my dad's finances, and she planned to remodel our little shack of a house. We needed temporary living quarters, so my mom approached the church and asked if she could rent the pastor's house behind the church since the church didn't have a full-time pastor. My mom worked out a deal with the church. We started packing up for the move when everything suddenly stopped. She was told that Reverend J. D. Harris objected to the deal and stopped the process, and I got highly upset and sought revenge.

Now, Reverend J. D. Harris was an actual ordained Baptist minister. He was also a gun-toting pimp, bootlegger, loan shark, and blackmailer, not to mention someone who could cook some of the best BBQ, collard greens, chitterlings, and cornbread ever. His speakeasy had two rooms for lounging, eating, and dancing. He was open some evenings during the week but always open on the weekends.

One day, I saw him leaving his house. I let him leave the yard, and he started walking down 4th Street toward Center Street so he would be gone for a while. I let him walk a couple of blocks away, and then I left my car and walked over to the steps that led up to a screened-in porch. I couldn't believe there was a lock on the porch door.

I went back to the car to grab my pry bar. I returned to the locked porch and pried open the screen porch door. I couldn't believe it again! The heavy-duty front door looked like something that belonged to Fort Knox. My pry bar was useless, so I left the screened-in porch and walked around the house. The back door was also an impenetrable metal door. All the basement windows had wire screens, and all the other windows were too high off the ground, and they, too, had heavy wire screens. Who was this dude? I was very upset. I left his property and went back to my car. I got in and sat stewing behind the wheel. I knew a huge payday was waiting for me, but I had no way to get into his house; it was so frustrating!

Time passed, and it looked like the deacons ignored the reverend's objection; they let my mom rent the pastor's house anyway. Day after day, it ate at me that the old fool was going to get away with what he did to my mom. J. D. Harris's house and speakeasy were around the corner from the church. Sometimes, I would walk to the end of the block, look across the street, and wonder how to get to him.

One day, I arrived at the pastor's house and overheard my mom talking on the phone. They were talking about an event at the Grange Hall, and I heard my mom say that old J. D. Harris would be there speaking. My ears perked up. When my mom was off the phone, I pressed her for more details. She verified that there was going to be a community event at the Grange Hall on Friday. Usually, I wanted to go because the variety of food at these events was always well worth the trip.

Friday came, and I must have been displaying signs of high anxiety because my brother asked me, "Okay, what's wrong with you? What's going on?" He also possessed an uncanny ability to read me, much like our mom. I told him how upset I was at J. D. Harris and how I had planned some payback. He told me he was also upset and asked what I was going to do. I told him about the frustrating things I had already done and my new plan: to hit the speakeasy while J. D. Harris and the rest of the community were at the Grange Hall.

My brother and I reviewed our plan Friday morning and agreed to meet at the pastor's house at 7 p.m. Since the event lasted from 7 to 10, I told my brother I was bringing a buddy.

My buddy and I made it to the pastor's house, and my brother was waiting. We hung out at the pastor's house until 8:00 p.m. We left the house, got into my 1957 Ford Fairlane station wagon, and drove to the alley behind J. D.'s speakeasy. No one was around, and fortunately, the back door to the speakeasy was a regular screen door and a regular back door, so it was fairly easy to breach both with my pry bar.

We broke in and immediately went to work. Junior searched for money and valuables while my buddy and I grabbed appliances and stuff we could sell. We took all the food—cooked, uncooked, and refrigerated. We took all the silverware, all the plastic and paper goods, including the toilet paper. We broke into the jukebox and took all the records and all the quarters. We broke into the booze room and took several cases of beer, wine coolers, and bottles of liquor. I even took a painting off the wall. The three of us moved like a well-oiled machine, and in half an hour, the cupboards were bare. We piled into the front seat of my wagon because every inch in the back of the station wagon was stuffed with the spoils of our treachery.

We drove out near Ross Park, where we divided a little over $600. We pulled up to a Dipsy Dumpster and got rid of stuff we didn't think we could sell. We stayed at the park for a while, gorging on ribs and bread and sucking down beer and wine coolers. We left the park and dropped off food to some welfare folks with their promise of silence.

It was around 11 p.m., so we decided to drive by the speakeasy, and my heart sank when we drove by. There were clusters of people standing around with long faces, doing absolutely nothing. I felt so bad as I looked at all the long, sad faces that had planned on eating, partying, and having fun, but that wouldn't happen since the "Grinch stole Christmas." There were other places for them to go, but going to the old geezer's speakeasy to party was a bit special, and the place always had a great atmosphere. Now, I felt strange about how my bitterness of revenge for the old man was being overshadowed with sorrow.

In my mind, I could hear my mom paraphrasing another bible verse, Romans 12:17, about not trading evil for evil. The proof was that my revenge backfired after seeing everyone standing around, and I couldn't rewind and erase the tape.

Gun Held to My Head

One day, walking home from school, I walked past the house of a star varsity football player who lived a block from the school. The varsity player stood in his doorway and called me over when he saw me. I walked over and stopped at the porch. He opened the door and said, "Come in and drop your bag." I did and followed him down a hallway into a room.

Four other varsity players were there, and he told me to sit down. They all were saying various things to me, and I began to think it was some type of initiation. Then I heard the other varsity players yell, "Hey man! What are you doing?" and "Put that away!" The big star varsity player stood behind me, and I couldn't see what was happening. I heard a rattling and clicking noise. Then, I heard the distinctive sound of a gun hammer falling.

I turned slightly and saw the gun in the big varsity player's hand. I tried to get up, but he grabbed me by the shoulder and forced me back down into the chair. He yelled at me, "Sit down, you little n****r and shut up!"

I heard the revolver cylinder spinning again, but the other varsity players jumped up, rushed, and stopped him. When his teammates rushed him, I jumped up, ran out of the room, grabbed my bag, and took off.

I don't know if the gun was loaded or not, but all I could think about was getting back at him. The next day, when I walked onto the school grounds, two varsity players who were in the house rushed up to me and apologized. They pleaded with me not to talk about the Russian Roulette game. I told them I wouldn't say anything as long as he left me alone, or else I would go to the police.

That Friday, in the dressing room after football practice, I overheard the idiot telling a teammate that he and his mother were going out of town for the weekend. As soon as I heard that, my mind jumped into payback mode.

That Friday evening, at about 10 p.m., I left the house with a flat-tip screwdriver and went to the idiot's mother's house. It was dark and quiet, so I walked around the side of the house to a basement window slightly cracked open, and there was a water spigot with an attached hose. I walked over to the window, used the screwdriver to poke a hole in the screen, guided the hose through the hole, turned the water on, and left.

The following Monday at school, I overheard the star varsity player angrily talking about how upset he was because his basement apartment was flooded, and my heart beamed with joy. Then he mentioned how upset his mother was, and my heart sank like a rock in his flooded apartment. For quite a while, all I could see in my mind were images of the poor mother, but I couldn't undo my wrong.

Pimps—Managers of Chaos

When I was in high school, I read a story about a pimp who used a devious tactic to condition a new girl he added to his flock. The tactic started with, over time, getting the girl strung out on booze, marijuana, cocaine, and eventually heroin. To establish her absolute dependence on him, he would choose a day when the girl was high and passed out. He'd pick her up and carry her to an open apartment window high above the street where he lived. Then he'd hang her body partly out the window and vigorously shake her. When the girl started to regain consciousness, she'd panic, realizing that she was hanging out a window high above the street.

When she was desperately begging the pimp to save her, he'd scream, "What the hell is wrong with you? Why are you trying to kill yourself?" Then he'd pull her from the window, carry her into the bedroom, and toss her on the bed. He'd take a wire hanger from the closet, pull it straight and long, and beat her "in the name of love"—a pimp's twisted creed. The pimp psychologically and emotionally owned her after that, and every future beating was done "in the name of love." When I read this, it blew my mind because I completely understood its treacherous, seductive power. It gave Mr. Hyde an evil tool.

After being depressed and confused for some time, I decided to take a break from college after completing two and a half years great years. I was randomly seeing a girl who I wasn't particularly fond of, but she liked me. She was a girl of means because her stepfather was a well-established businessman in Pocatello, and they lived up on "The Hill." She drove a brand-new car and always had plenty of money.

One evening, we were partying at her house while her parents were gone. I awakened after passing out. As I lay on her king-size bed, I wondered why I wasn't still in school, why I didn't go into the Air Force, why I didn't move to Seattle, and on and on. I became upset. Suddenly, I remembered the story about the pimp and the girl, and a dark idea came to me as I glanced over at the girl lying next to me.

I rolled off the bed, walked over to a table, and picked up a single-edged razor blade we were using. I took it to the bathroom and laid it on the floor. Then, I returned to the bedroom, picked up the girl's limp body, carried her to the bathroom, and positioned both of us on the bathroom floor.

I picked up the razor blade, made several shallow cuts on her left wrist, and squeezed her arm until blood appeared. I placed the razor blade between her thumb and forefinger on her right hand and held her hand with my left hand. I began to shake and yell at her until she finally came to. When she opened her eyes and saw the blood, she instantly panicked and freaked out. I yelled, "Are you crazy? Why are you trying to kill yourself?"

I shook the razor blade out of her hand as she laid on the bedroom floor. She frantically rolled around the floor, crying uncontrollably. I picked her up, carried her back to the bedroom, and tossed her on the bed. There was a trickle of blood running down her arm, but it might as well have been major hemorrhaging the way she was carrying on. I thought about getting a coat hanger or maybe a belt to beat her in dedication to the pimp's creed, "in the name of love," but because she was completely out of control, I thought it was best to calm her down and treat her wounds. Then I said, "You better be glad I was here to save you from yourself." I stayed long enough to calm her down, and then I left.

As time passed, she began showing up everywhere. I would drive up to my mom's house, and she would be waiting for me. Even though I would sometimes hook up with her for a short while and then leave her, she would continue to follow me like a shadow.

One day, I got fed up, screamed, and yelled at her to leave me alone. A few days passed, and I didn't see or hear from her. I soon heard that one of her girlfriends had discovered her after attempting to commit suicide, and she was recovering in the hospital.

A chill ran through me when I heard the numbing news, and I was sure I had something to do with it. Unlike a pimp who would stick around to manage the chaos he had created; I completely abandoned my victim. I immediately realized that I was no pimp, and I concluded that I had probably set her up for a real mental breakdown.

Not long after I heard the news about the girl, my mom mentioned it one morning while we ate breakfast. She said, "That girl who would sit out front waiting for you? I heard she was up in Bannock Hospital recovering from a suicide attempt."

What could I say? I sat there feeling empty as my mom stared at me. I could tell she knew something was up, but there was no way I could tell her the truth. I thought brainwashing was just an ambiguous term. What the pimp did and what I attempted to copy was very real. How wrong I was about brainwashing and stooping to such a devious tactic.

Ripped-Off Croc

I had known TC all my life, and now I knew him as a big-time dealer. TC pushed a bit of everything, but he mainly dealt from ounces to kilos of prime Idaho green, Acapulco gold, Colombian gold, Thai stick, vials of hashish, large quantities of acid, Mescaline, and sheets of opium.

One day, TC introduced me to an interesting guy whom I called Croc. I gave him the nickname because he looked like the folk singer Jim Croce, plus he had a weird last name that I continuously destroyed. Croc had a master's degree in some field of nuclear engineering, and he had an office at the Engineering Test Reactor (ETR) site. Croc and I grew very close. He invited me to his house one evening after work, stating that he had something interesting to show me. After about an hour of reviewing the information he had, he asked me if I wanted to go over to TC's, and I agreed, so we took off in our individual cars.

When we arrived, "Do What You Like" by Blind Faith was blasting. We were invited in, offered drinks, and pointed to a candy dish full of rolled joints. I made myself at home, and TC called Croc into the kitchen. After a short while, I saw Croc put a jar of Orange Sunshine acid in a paper bag before they walked out of the kitchen. We stayed at TC's for a while and eventually went our separate ways.

The next evening after work, I called Croc to see if he was home. He didn't answer the phone. I jumped in my car and raced over to TC's house first. Croc's car was parked outside, so I raced over to Croc's house. I saw the light on in the living room, so I parked, got out of the car, walked to the door, and knocked because sometimes his girlfriend was at the house. The front door was locked, so I walked around to the back door, and it was unlocked. I opened the door, entered the screened-in porch area, and walked through the unlocked kitchen door. I cautiously opened the door, slowly walked in, and called out, but no one answered.

I walked straight to the bedroom, and in the dim light, I felt my way to the closet. My first guess was correct. The jar was on the top shelf, so I grabbed it and exited the house. My mind was flooded with a vision of Croc. A tape started playing in my head, scenes of enjoyable times I spent with him. The guy even co-signed a re-fi for my car. Even though my car was almost paid off, he still stuck his neck out for me. Man! My heart was so heavy. I felt terrible. I thought, *"Why am I doing this to him?"* But Mr. Hyde convinced me to keep the jar of acid.

Time passed, and I hadn't seen Croc for a while. My guilt led me to avoid him. I discovered he had not been at work because he left with the FBI one day. I found out he had been relieved of his security clearance and position. I didn't want to think if it had anything to do with my ripping him off. I went over to TC's, and Black Sabbath was blasting with a heavy party going on. TC was in the kitchen, so I went to him and asked, "Hey man, have you seen Croc?"

He said, "Aw man, he got busted. That day, when you guys came over, he picked up a jar of Orange Sunshine and got ripped off before he settled with the suppliers, and they got very upset. They dropped a bomb on him, and when the cops raided his house, they found a variety of other stuff, so he got arrested, lost his security clearance, lost his job, and his girlfriend left him. Man, he lost everything!"

A shock wave stormed through me. I asked TC, "He got the jar from you. So, are you okay with the suppliers?"

He said, "Yeah, I only delivered the goods. They were the dudes from Sun Valley, and those dudes don't play around."

I walked back into the living room for a few minutes and left. When I got outside, I walked around to the side of the house, got sick to my stomach, and threw up. I couldn't believe what TC said. It *was* all my fault. I started crying like a baby and convulsing, and I threw up again. I hated myself. My mind was flooded with images of Croc, flashing images of the two of us when we were together. I wanted to crawl out of my skin, but I couldn't get away from the evil, dreadful Mr. Hyde influence buried within me. The terrible, destructive situation that I put such an outstanding person in left me despising myself. After a while, I slowly started to gather myself. I made my way to my car with puke still all over my shoes, but I didn't care.

I tried to justify my actions with the reason that he got caught up in the hustle of the dog-eat-dog drug world, and it's part of the game about getting over or getting done or getting ripped off. But if that was the case, why did I still feel so terrible, and why was it still lying so heavily on my mind and heart? Croc was all I could regretfully think about for a very long time.

The Plant Director's Heart

I was working for a great computer repair company, and I not only became a premier employee for my manager but also caught the attention of the shop's director, who thanked me for all of my organization and hard work. Despite the great things going on, a dark cloud was looming. For every positive step Dr. Jekyll took, Mr.

Hyde was always right behind him to trip him up. Along with my leadership position came special privileges that I abused.

My decision to assist in pilfering expensive items was the setup for a tragic episode for me, letting down my wife, my girls, my manager, and the director. I got arrested and, in the process, destroyed the makings of a great career. I imagined how disappointed my mother would be in me. I further thought about how disappointed the judge, the Gunny, and my recruiter would be, not to mention my 4 Crusaders, who definitely wouldn't have done what I did.

Once again, there I was, in another one of the pitifully destructive seasons of my life, and once again, my mother's Grace of God showed up with another miracle. The upper management in New York wasn't pleased with how the director handled the situation. About a month after my arrest, I was called for a meeting with the shop's human relations director. I was informed that all charges against me were dropped, and my bail was refunded. I also received retro pay and additional restitution compensation. It appeared that my life was miraculously back on track again.

Time passed, and I received a phone call from a technician who used to work for me. He told me the shop director suffered a heart attack shortly after New York dismissed him. He was bedridden for a while, and then he told me he had died. I immediately felt sick to my stomach. I said goodbye, hung up, and went upstairs to the bathroom.

When I entered the bathroom, my knees buckled. I immediately grew numb as I broke down in tears. I leaned against the wall and slid to the floor, crying uncontrollably and feeling empty. The HR director said nothing about the director's heart attack. Here I was again, feeling terrible, and I couldn't escape from myself. I kept rewinding the tape in my head to the last time the plant director rewarded me. I finally stopped crying, and an image of my mother flooded my mind as I imagine to asked her, "Will God forgive me for setting the guy up for a heart attack and now responsible for his death?" I felt that even though I didn't pull the trigger, I was holding the smoking gun.

FACING MY DEMONS

On to Step 5 *(Cleaning House—Spiritual Regurgitation)*

I was supposed to meet Doug at the restaurant, and this meeting would be very different from the rest. Normally, I would be extremely anxious to meet Doug and get to the restaurant early, but I don't know why I was so apprehensive this time. We agreed to meet at 1 p.m., but I decided to lay down a little afternoon and take a nap. It was 1:45 p.m. when I woke up. I lay in bed thinking to myself that I had blown it. Doug would probably not be there if I were to leave and go to the restaurant. I decided to get up and go anyway. I arrived at about 2:15 p.m. I walked through the door, and the girl behind the reception counter pointed to the back corner, and there he was.

As I started walking toward him, he was laughing as usual. We shared greetings, shook hands, and Doug said, "So, you had a little problem getting here?"

I felt he knew I had planned the stalling tactic, and he continued laughing as we sat down and went to work.

Step 5: Admitted to God, ourselves, and another human being the exact nature of our wrongs. The *Twelve Steps and Twelve Traditions* book states, "What we receive from Step 5 is the beginning of true kinship with man and God. Losing the sense of isolation, receiving forgiveness, and giving it; learning humility; gaining honesty and realism about ourselves, which is a necessity for complete honesty."

Doug looked and said, "Well, tell me your story."

I opened my notebook and started reading.

He interrupted me. "You don't have to read word-for-word. Give me the main details."

I spent the next three hours telling Doug about stealing and wrecking my dad's car, Indian Girl's death, driving Old Man Robertson crazy and out of town, robbing J. D. Harris, flooding the house, Razor Blade Girl, how Croc lost everything, Plant Director's heart attack, burglarizing houses and businesses, robbing innocent people, violating several girls, allowing others to take the fall for me, stealing several vehicles, violating one of my mom's female friends, violating a girlfriend's mother, stealing from the neighbors, a buddy was incarcerated instead of me, and on and on.

My emotions and my heart became extremely heavy during my confession. Several times, I couldn't do anything but cry, and Doug would calm and comfort me with some of his horror stories. I thought I had done some terrible things, but Doug told me things that made me look like a church choir boy. Doug was a heaven-sent sponsor, and I honestly believe I couldn't have done this with anyone else.

I felt absolutely wonderful when we finished. When I left, it was as if I was floating across the parking lot to my car. As I sat in my car, my heart felt liberated, then suddenly, I plunged into a deep, dark, heavy state of depression and disappointment. I sat there, feeling miserable, as I thought, *You don't deserve this great feeling of relief and peace when there were people who were hurt and lost their lives because of you. How dare you feel any sense of jubilation with your blood-stained hands.* I sat behind the wheel of my car, feeling weak and empty, and I didn't know what to do.

On to Step 6 *(Willingness to Stop Struggling)*

A couple of days after meeting Doug at the restaurant, I felt in my mind, heart, and soul that I had truly advanced to a point where I was feeling whole again. I began to feel like someone with something good and positive to offer to others besides my usual destructive behavior. But soon I would slip into a deep depression again.

I continued attending AA meetings, but I had not seen Doug for a while. My sharing in the meetings must have sounded a bit peculiar to some because I was approached by a few people after meetings, and they expressed their concern about what I was sharing. My current state of mind was confusion and depression after the downward crash from Step 5 sharing with Doug. I was lost, and I didn't know what to do, but I didn't feel like drinking. I was beginning to worry more since Doug wasn't around.

One afternoon, I walked out of a meeting, and Scott, one of my close AA associates, stopped and said, "Hey there, what's going on with you?"

I asked Scott if he had seen Doug. He said he heard that Doug went back East to visit relatives.

I got upset. *How dare he leave and not tell me?* Then, I realized that it was none of my business, so I left it alone.

Scott asked me again, "What's going on? I can tell there's something wrong."

I explained what happened after my Step 5: "Moral Inventory" with Doug.

Scott said, "Well, it looks like you need to move on to Step 6 and Step 7. Do you want me to help you?

I shrugged. "Sure, why not?"

We agreed to meet at a local Denny's restaurant.

I arrived early, so I went inside and got a booth. When Scott arrived, we reviewed Step 6: We're entirely ready to have God remove all these defects of character. Scott mentioned that outside Step 3, Step 6 is probably the next most spiritual step. The 12/12 Book states that the Grace of God can forgive our derelictions as we surrender our will to God's will, and acceptance is the key. The power of God's Grace can supernaturally remove the mania from our alcohol-driven lives. The Grace of God's spirit can enter and expel all obsessions and help us accept and forgive ourselves for the wake of the destruction we created in our past.

Scott understood Step 6 extremely well, and I got it. That's when my depressive bubble began to pop. I understood why I was struggling after my Step 5 regurgitation with Doug. I was truly sorrowful and regretful for the things I had done. I understood the change in me was more than emotional; it was spiritual, and I was already surrendering to God's will with Steps 4 and 5 and opening up to His forgiveness. Now, I must accept my past, not dwell upon it, and let it go.

Scott and I met one more time the following week. That meeting was remarkably interesting. When we met, Scott conducted a Step 6 test with a barrage of questions. I responded well because when we were through, Scott said, "I think you're ready to move on to Step 7."

I answered, "Yes, I think I got it. It's God's will and not my will. Stop worrying, stop the internal struggle, let go of my past, and move on."

I suddenly understood why we repeated the Serenity Prayer in the meetings: "God grant me the serenity to accept the things I cannot change, courage to change the things I can, and the wisdom to know the difference." I thought, *Okay, I've got to let go and move on.*

On to Step 7 (*God Help Me to Drop My Pride and Let Go*)

Step 6 was nothing less than amazing! I never knew there was something that would make such a huge difference in my life. I was in so much pain over the many destructive things I had done to people. I found myself desperately willing to surrender to the one thing my mom constantly talked about: the Grace of God.

I honestly didn't know what it was, but something was stirring deep within me, and I believe it was a spiritual seed planted by my mother's faith, something that was urging me to open my mind, my heart, and my soul to what God's Grace had in store for me. So, I was truly dealing with something supernatural.

I was beginning to feel that it was a blessing that Doug was gone, and that Scott was around to take his place. Scott was able to convey Step 6 concepts to me in a way that I clearly understood. Not that Doug probably couldn't do the same, but it was vividly different from Scott. I didn't know what to expect from Step 7, but I was hoping for more good things like what happened in Step 6, such as the heavy depression going away. I was still sorry for my past, but thinking about it no longer pulled me down into a deep, dark hole of misery and sorrow.

Step 7: Humbly ask Him to remove our shortcomings. I thought, *So, I am supposed to humble myself and ask God to do something?* AA introduced me to the Seven Deadly Sins of pride, greed, lust, anger, gluttony, envy, and slothfulness, and my mind instantly migrated to the number one deadly sin of pride when I first read about them. My pride had always been my shield. My pride had always been my Mr. Hyde enabler, which justified me in doing whatever I chose.

Before meeting Scott, I read Step 7. I recalled reading about striving for greater humility and avoiding highlighting my pride in my achievements. Scott and I met again at Denny's. We read through Step 7 again, and then we held a lengthy discussion. After about three hours, Scott helped me come to an understanding that the willingness I gained in Step 6 placed me in the midst of Step 7. When my pride withered away, I was left sitting in remorseful pain in my car after sharing Step 5 with Doug.

I finished Step 7 with greater spiritual jubilation than I completed Step 6 with. But Scott told me that if I was supposedly at a point of true humility, honesty, and surrendering my will, then I should also be at a point where I was willing to let go of my past and move on. I wholeheartedly agree. Scott also warned me that there would be people who would be unhappy with me and probably even hate or despise me, but that is what Steps 8 and 9 are all about: making amends. I should be aware that I would never be able to please or be forgiven by everyone; all I could do was cling to the Serenity Prayer, drop the rock, and move on.

On to Step 8 *(Making Amends List)*

I met with Scott again a couple of days after our Step 7 meeting. In preparation for our Step 8 meeting, I started plowing through my Step 4 inventory in my notebook. I started creating a list of names with a comment summarizing my interaction with them. Everybody appeared approachable until I got to the names of those who were no longer here. Remembering some of these folks left me a little empty, but I was all right. But this time, recalling the names and faces of some of my past victims did not throw me into a deep depression like before Step 6. To be conscious and not have the depressive weight and pressure of guilt, regret, and remorse cloaking me like a heavy, dark shroud. Working these steps up to this point enables me to believe that I can, once again, become a positive contributing member of society.

On to Step 9 *(Asking for Forgiveness)*

It took about a week to complete my list, and then I called Scott to set up a meeting at Denny's.

Step 9: Make direct amends to such people wherever possible, except when doing so would injure them or others. The problem with Step 9 is that several people I needed to make amends with were back in Pocatello, starting with my mother, but there were several people in California to start with.

The main consideration for Step 9 is to discuss every proposed case with your AA sponsor thoroughly. Scott and I discussed my possible cases and summarized a long list into a shorter one. Scott said to call him before I approached anyone. I didn't follow Scott's advice and learned a hard lesson.

I heard that one of my previous managers was leaving the company. I thought this guy if anybody, would be open and receptive to my apology, which I planned to present to him with great care. I thought for sure that once he saw the change in me, he would be supportive of the change in me. When he was my manager, I was always buzzed, missing work, and barely hanging on by a thread. Much like a story in the Big Book, I told this manager that if I didn't straighten up and fly right, he should fire me, or I would quit on my own because he had me on the final written warning.

I went to his office to make amends. I knocked on the open door and waited.

He glanced up from his desk but didn't invite me in, so I stepped inside the open door. "Hello, Tan. I wanted to stop by to talk to you, so do you have a moment or two?"

He looked up and said, "I have nothing to say to you. Goodbye."

I was in shock as I turned around and left his office. I was embarrassed and hurt as I walked down the hallway. Wow! Scott was right. There would be some people suffering from irreversible damage. I didn't contact Scott first about this manager, and I am pretty sure that Scott would have probably told me to skip him. But I didn't follow his instructions and paid the emotional price. I always contacted Scott first after my painful manager fiasco.

On to Step 10 *(Keep a Check on Myself)*

Step 10: Continue to take personal inventory, and when we are wrong, promptly admit it.

It didn't take long to read Step 10 again, and the step was very straightforward to me, being about continued willingness, a willingness to strive for better things, a willingness to admit when I'm at fault, and a willingness to forgive when the fault is on others. A key to maintaining a quality life in recovery is a willingness to administer self-care and self-awareness. A critical tool I was taught in AA to help with this and to stay ahead of the temptation to drink was an aid known as HALT, which stands for Hungry, Angry, Lonely, Tired. Any time recovering alcoholics find themselves simultaneously under any two of the states, there is reason for heightened attention, awareness, and recovery action. Any time recovering alcoholics find themselves simultaneously under any three or all four of the states, there is reason for alarm, and they should immediately reach out for help. So, to me, Step 10 was like a self-monitoring radar that was always on.

On to Step 11 (Growing Closer to My God)

It was late Sunday evening. The girls were in bed, and Deby and I had a very pleasant conversation. This was so different, being at home in peace. Deby got up and went to the bedroom. I grabbed my 12/12 book and sat down to read Step 11.

Step 11: Sought through prayer and meditation to improve our conscious contact with God as we understood Him, praying only for knowledge of His will for us and the power to carry that out.

When I finished reading about midnight, I leaned back and relaxed in my seat, overcome with a huge feeling of gratitude. A few months earlier, I was drowning in my craziness because I couldn't stop drinking and drugging, and there were times when I even contemplated suicide because I couldn't stop. I didn't know what to do and didn't want to go on.

I recalled what occurred early one Saturday morning, February 20, 1993, when I had a vision of my mother. I also heard the 23rd Psalm echo in my head and flashes of my 4 Crusaders. I'd cried out, "God, please help me! Jesus, what am I supposed to do?" Then, something came over me, and I was instantaneously, miraculously, supernaturally rendered clean and sober. It was amazing, and it was a miracle!

After my spiritual awakening, I had a thirst for spiritual knowledge. I remembered a book I used to read during my college days. The book was *The Prophet* by Kahlil Gibran. I went to the garage, searched through some boxes, and found it. Then, I rushed back into the house and started reading it.

Monday morning, I made it to work with *The Prophet*. I was highly intrigued by the book, so I sat down and started reading it before work. I was sharing a cube space with a lady named Terry.

Terry entered the cube. "Good morning," she said.

I responded in kind and approached her with the book in hand. "Terry, check this out," and I read a segment about children to her:

Your children are not your children. They are the sons and daughters of life's longing for itself. They come through you but not from you, and though they are with you, yet they belong not to you (Knopf, 1923).

Terry replied. "That's nice, but if you want to read something enlightening, you need to read the bible."

"Okay, but I don't have a bible."

Terry and I had worked together for quite a while. She worked in a strained environment because she constantly had to deal with the side effects of my alcohol and drug issues. However, our relationship changed drastically when she saw that my sobriety was truly the order of the day for me.

We began talking regularly. Terry told me about the bible. I told her I was raised a Southern Baptist, and my mother always read the bible to me and my siblings. She told me she was raised as a Christian and attended a church called Calvary Chapel of Costa Mesa.

Lunchtime rolled around, so I left my lab and returned to my cube. In the past, I would have taken off to my favorite Pizza Hut and consumed my usual two liters of rose wine and maybe some pizza for a two-plus-hour lunch. In my new sobriety, I would grab my books and go to the cafeteria to read and eat, then head back to work after my hour-long lunch, but when I arrived back at the cube, Terry was sitting at her desk. As I entered the cube area, she excitedly jumped up.

She rushed up to me. "Here, I have a gift for you!"

I took the sack from her, opened it, and took out a book. It was a Sobriety Bible. This blew my mind. Not only did I get a bible, but it was also associated with the AA 12-Step Book. I thanked Terry and gave her a big hug. Then, I returned the bible to the sack since the workday wasn't over. I was extremely excited and couldn't wait to get home with my new bible.

Before we left work that day, Terry also gave me a cassette tape titled "Monuments: Sacred or Profane?" She said it was a bible study out of the book of Isaiah by Chuck Missler and it was a techy type of study that I would truly enjoy. She shared that Chuck Missler was the CEO of WD in the mid-to-late seventies, and he'd brought the company out of bankruptcy. Eventually, the tape led me to attend live bible studies at Calvary Chapel of Costa Mesa, where my Step 11 conscience contact with God truly started.

18

AA LED ME TO THE CHAPEL

I Found My Home Church

My first experience at Calvary Chapel Costa Mesa (CCCM) was amazing. I attended a Chuck Missler study, picked up a church bulletin, and read through it. I saw there was a bible study every night of the week except for Saturday. There were even bible studies and prayer meetings in a variety of languages. This place was amazing.

I saw an AA program called "One Step Program" listed in the bulletin, and I started attending the program meetings on Wednesday nights. It was far different from the AA meetings I was used to attending, so one Wednesday, I decided to leave the meeting.

Normally, I parked my car outside the classroom door where the meeting was held at the back of CCCM High School. This particular evening, I'd left my car parked at the front of the church across from the bookstore. As I was walking from the classroom, I could hear music and singing as I entered the plaza area. It was filled with people sitting and watching big-screen TVs mounted on the side of the main chapel. I continued walking and eventually reached the main chapel main entrance. I was suddenly compelled to open a door. I walked into the familiar lobby area, where an usher handed me a bulletin before entering the main chapel. As I walked through the door, I heard the big, booming voice of Pastor David Hocking say, "Welcome to the book of Genesis." Something rushed through me, and I knew I was where I was supposed to be.

I started attending a bible study Monday through Friday and was especially drawn to Monday nights with Pastor Greg Laurie's bible study, which pulled in a younger crowd. I joined the Discipleship

Ministry, the follow-up ministry for the Greg Laurie Bible Study. An outstanding pastor headed the Discipleship Ministry. Pastor Dave introduced me to spiritual warfare based on Ephesians 6: 10–12.

[10] Finally, my brethren, be strong in the Lord and the power of His might. [11]Put on the whole armor of God, that you may be able to stand against the wiles of the devil. [12]For we do not wrestle against flesh and blood, but against principalities, against powers, against the rulers of the darkness of this age, against spiritual hosts of wickedness in the heavenly places.

Pastor Dave warned us about attacks from Satan's evil spiritual realm, and he was right because several strange things occurred during some of our meetings.

First Calvary Chapel Men's Conference

October rolled around, and the church bulletin listed the CCCM Men's Conference at the Anaheim Convention Center. I had no idea what it was, but I attended anyway. Pastor Chuck hosted and spoke at the conference with other speakers, Jon Courson, Steve Mays, Mike MacIntosh, and several other Calvary Chapel pastors. This is where I received Jesus Christ as my Lord and Savior, the direct execution of scripture Romans 10: 9 "[9]That if you confess with your mouth the Lord Jesus and believe in your heart that God has raised Him from the dead, you will be saved."

I expanded my church attendance after the CCCM Men's Conference. I started attending Prophecy Conferences, mini–Men's Conferences, and presentations at Calvary Chapels all over Orange and LA Counties. Meanwhile, Deby and the girls were attending a small church in Tustin, and she refused to attend CCCM with me. Later, she finally allowed me to start taking our daughters to the mid-Sunday service at CCCM, but she still refused to go. I began to sense something was wrong and had no idea what it was.

One Sunday, during Pastor Chuck's middle service, he said something that caught my attention: "Your family is your first ministry." That Wednesday evening during Pastor David Hocking's study, I heard it again: "Your family is your first ministry." Then it hit me. I was moving on, but I was leaving my family behind. Even though I was taking the girls to Pastor Chuck's mid-Sunday service, Deby and the girls were not my priority; they were not my first ministry. I immediately closed my bible and notebook, got up, and left the study. As I walked to my car, I could only think about Deby. An image of her sitting at home alone was stuck in my mind. I couldn't wait to get home and talk to her.

I didn't remember driving home. I drove in some weird, suspended mental state since all I could think about and all I could see was my wife. I eventually pulled up in front of the house and parked. I scrambled out of the car, ran to the front door, rushed into the house, and there she was. She was sitting alone on the couch. It was about 8:45 p.m., and the girls were in bed, so the timing was perfect for Deby and me to have a nice, sincere talk. She stared at me as I walked over and sat beside her. I reached over and gently picked up her hands, and I looked into her eyes and said, "I know you are happy that I'm no longer carousing around drinking, drugging, and acting a fool, right?"

She replied, "Yes, I am."

I asked, "But even though I am no longer out there, I'm still not here either, correct?"

She replied, "Yes, between your work and church, you are never here with me and the girls."

"Then, you have the same problem with me not being here, minus the alcohol and drugs, right?"

She replied, "Yes, your church has become your new alcohol and drug."

Wow! What she said was crushing but true. I now clearly understood what and where my first ministry was: my family. I told her I would no longer attend all the bible studies, conferences, and special church events. I asked if she would attend CCCM with me, and she agreed. We became a church-attending family.

Learning God's Holy Scripture Was the Key

In a few months, I learned a lot at CCCM. I had learned about the Jesus that my mother believed in, the Jesus she strove so hard to teach me about, the Jesus she said everybody needs. Not only did I attend the church, but I also listened to the church radio station KWAVE 107.9 FM, listening to other great pastors like Pastor Chuck Smith, Jon Courson, Greg Laurie, Steve Mays, David Rosales, Raul Ries, Vernon McGee, Chuck Swindoll, Tony Evans, and many more outstanding pastors, and currently being taught by my wonderfully anointed Pastor Barry Stagner.

I learned about biblical doctrines, such as propitiation, justification, sanctification, and glorification, and I understood these particular doctrines as the steppingstones to eternal salvation. But one of the most important concepts I learned was that Christianity is not a religion; it's about developing a personal relationship with the only true living God through the acceptance of Jesus Christ as my Lord and Savior which is enabled by the supernatural power of the Holy Spirit tugging on my heartstrings.

That relationship was initially revealed to me with the understanding of John 3:16 (For God so loved the world that He gave His only begotten Son, that whoever believes in Him should not perish but have everlasting life). But then I asked myself, How do I go about believing in what for everlasting life? What to believe was again revealed to me in Romans 10:9–10 (9that if you confess with your mouth the Lord Jesus and believe in your heart that God has raised Him from the dead, you will be saved. 10For with the heart one believes unto righteousness, and with the mouth confession is made unto salvation.)

This being saved drove me to a very basic question: Why am I here in the first place if I have to be saved? I learned that we are all here because God simply wanted us, as revealed in Colossians 1:16 (For by Him, all things were created that are in heaven and that are on earth, visible and invisible, whether thrones or dominions or principalities or powers. All things were created through Him and for Him.). And we are here for Him to work His will in us and for His pleasure as revealed in Philippians 2:13 ("For it is God who works in you both to will and to do for *His* good pleasure.")

So, I ask myself, If we are here for God's pleasure, then what was Jesus Christ dying on the cross all about? I learned that the short answer was because of sin. In 1 Peter 1:16 ("···because it is written, 'Be holy, for I am holy.'"), we who exist for God's good pleasure are supposed to be holy as God is Holy. But God's holiness means He is transcendent, incomprehensible, and uniquely glorious that He cannot be fully measured, so where does that leave us unholy sin-ridden beings in his creation?

I learned that in the Old Testament, the blood from animal sacrifice was used to atone for the sins of unholy man. Blood was the required payment for sin, as expressed in Leviticus 17:11 ("For the life of the flesh *is* in the blood, and I have given it to you upon the altar to make atonement for your souls; for it *is* the blood *that* makes atonement for the soul."). Then, I wanted to know if blood sacrifice was required forever. History states that blood sacrifice started in the Old Testament but ended around AD70 when the Roman army destroyed the Temple in Jerusalem. But, on top of that, the blood sacrificial system was adamantly done away with between AD30 and AD33 when the blood of Jesus Christ was the ultimate blood sacrifice on the cross and was the atonement for all sin, as revealed in John 19:30 ("So when Jesus had received the sour wine, He said, 'It is finished!' and bowing His head, He gave up His spirit.")

So, the priesthood and the sacrificial system were immediately obsolete, as alluded to in Matthew 27:51 ("Then, behold, the veil of the temple was torn in two from top to bottom, and the earth quaked, and the rocks were split"). The veil separated the innermost area of the temple (Holy of Holies), which only the High Priest was allowed to access. It represented the separation between sinful man and Holy God, so when the veil was torn in half, man was no longer separated from God, anyone and everyone was granted full access to God.

Since learning that confessing Jesus is my Lord, believing in my heart that God raised Him from the dead, and knowing that I have full access to God, I learned that I have a different spirit living within, me as just as Jesus told the Pharisees Nicodemus, in John 3:3 ("Jesus answered and said to him, 'Most assuredly, I say to you, unless one is born again, he cannot see the kingdom of God.') Upon my confession, I was born with God's spirit reining within me.

And now, with God's spirit reigning within me, I can benefit from the fruit of the spirit as stated in Galatians 5:22–23 ("But the fruit of the Spirit is love, joy, peace, longsuffering, kindness, goodness, faithfulness, 23gentleness, self-control. Against such there is no law.") And unlike my alcoholic imprisoned days, I can now present a better character to the world by yielding to scripture like Philippians 4:5 ("Let your gentleness be known to all men. The Lord *is* at hand.") And I can strive for real peace by yielding to scripture like Romans 12:18 ("If it is possible, as much as depends on you, live peaceably with all men."). My life is so different because I yielded to God's powerful word working within me.

CHAPTER

19

MY MOTHER WAS RIGHT

My Mother Told Me It Was All About Jesus

Looking back, I have no doubt whatsoever that my mother was right about everything she told me. I often wonder what direction my life would have taken if I had been more obedient and compliant while I was growing up. Then again, if my life had taken a different path, I would not have gone through all of the life-shaping times and experiences that molded me into who I am today, nor would I be able to share this memoir.

I remember attending church and reading the bible throughout my junior high school years. However, my life became busier and more complicated during high school, so attending church and reading the bible were no longer my priorities. Still, my mother remained faithful, attending church and reading her bible. My church attendance and reading of the bible were nonexistent by the time college rolled around, but my mother remained faithful to both.

When I think about my mother and how steady she remained after all I had put her through, I have concluded that motherhood was the toughest job in the world. Regardless of my mother's circumstances, she still had to be all things at all times for her children. Where dads were the head of the family, mothers were the heartbeats that kept family life and family love flowing through the home. When I think about how God watched over my mother, I think about the poem written by William Ross Wallace, "The Hand That Rocks the Cradle." He wrote, "Blessings on the hand of women! Angels guard its strength and grace," and I think about how unaware I was as my mom's hand and her spiritual influence shadowed over my life. Then, when he wrote, "For the hand that rocks the cradle is the hand that rules the world," I think about how my destructive life eventually turned around due to my mother's dedication to God, Jesus, the Holy Spirit, the bible, and not giving up on me.

Once sobriety became the norm for me, I started to see the real world around me. I would think about my mother's big-picture outlook on life and society, which made me think about a quote from Noah Webster: "All the miseries and evils which men suffer from vice, crime, ambition, injustice, oppression, slavery and war, proceed from their despising or neglecting the precepts contained in the bible."

My mom would simply put it, "White folks are caught up in too many White folk's things, and Black folks are caught up in too many Black folk's things, and everyone needs to understand how much God truly loves them all and how everyone needs to follow His Word."

And Pastor Tony Evans best describes it today, "Anglo Christians have wrapped their faith in the American flag and have developed a Christian nationalism that is foreign to scripture, and Black Christians tend to wrap our faith in Black culture so that if it's Black and we feel it, it must be biblical."

On the grand scales of race, religion, and culture, people have not been able to come together on a standard understanding or belief that would bring all people together in true peace and harmony. I have concluded that my mother was right and in agreement with Webster and Pastor Evans, and that standard must be based on the Word of God.

I used to be a person who would steal a $100 bill from you and then turn around and help you look for it. I looked at using people as a means to fulfill my needs and desires. However, I ultimately changed because I started to depend upon what my mother depended upon, and that was total trust and faith in the Spirit of God and the Word of God.

There were things my mother would repeatedly say, and those same things need to be repeated in homes, in political circles, and throughout American culture. Those things she used to say were words of enlightenment like "Believe in the Lord," "Trust in the

Lord," and "Wait on the Lord." They were spiritually charged words that would haunt me when Mr. Hyde exerted his influence upon me, and my pride would take over as I was on my way to executing some dastardly deeds. I eventually accepted that her words about the Lord possessed a supernatural power. I would begin to think how unfortunate it was that my mom's words were foreign to people who didn't believe in the only true living God and the Holy Scriptures. Scripture that would fill the spiritual voids that Noah Webster and Tony Evans alluded to.

My mother was on target to continuously question me throughout the decades about my lack of church attendance and not reading my bible. Alexis de Tocqueville, a nineteenth-century French historian, sums it up in his greatest quote: "I sought for the greatness and genius of America in her democratic Congress and her matchless Constitution, and it was not there. Not until I went into the churches of America and heard her pulpits flame with righteousness did I understand the secret of her genius and power. America is great because she is good, and if America ever ceases to be good, she will cease to be great." I'm not sure if my mother even knew who Alexis de Tocqueville was, but she understood what he stressed about losing true greatness. I spent decades fighting against God's supernatural providence because I simply didn't understand the nature of the spiritual warfare that was being battled in America's pulpits. Today, I focus on trying to live in that greatness that the historian and my mother understood.

I have learned it's about the power behind God's spirit changing my natural spirit. With that change in my spirit came a change in my soul, which influenced a change in my mind, propagating a change in my thinking and spawning a change in my behavior and actions. My mother would have put it in more direct terms, "Boy, if you quit thinking like the devil, you'll quit acting like the devil."

Today, I get it. I purpose in my heart to walk in faith in the Lord Jesus and to believe, trust, and wait on the Lord, just like my mom. Like my mom, I seek to strive and thrive in God's love, grace, mercy, and peace, and my mom was right all along; there is power in the name of Jesus and His Word.